RIGBY
On Our Way to English®

Activity Book

Rigby®

HOUGHTON MIFFLIN HARCOURT

Contents

Contents

Contents

NAME _____

WHAT TO DO

If you can't think of a word . . .

point.   **make a gesture.**   **draw a picture.**

say it another way.

ELPS 1.C use strategies to acquire vocabulary • 1.D speak using learning strategies • 1.H develop repertoire of learning strategies • 2.D.2 seek clarification of spoken language • 2.E.1 use visual support to enhance understanding • 2.I.1 demonstrate listening comprehension by following directions

NAME _____

WAYS TO HELP

Be patient:

- with your words.
- with your expression.
- with your attitude.

Watch for cues:

- in actions.
- in gestures.
- in expressions.

Be encouraging by:

- asking questions.
- giving support.

ELPS 1.C use strategies to acquire vocabulary • 1.D speak using learning strategies • 1.H develop repertoire of learning strategies • 2.D.2 seek clarification of spoken language as needed • 2.E.1 use visual support to enhance understanding • 3.B.3 use routine language for classroom communication • 3.F.1 ask for information

NAME _____

WHAT TO DO

If you don't understand . . .

sit close to the teacher.

ask questions.

Sorry, I didn't understand. Could you repeat that more slowly?

ask the speaker to slow down.

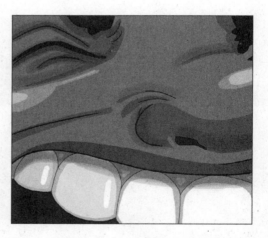

watch the speaker's mouth.

- This will help you understand.

- It will also help you with your pronunciation.

ELPS 1.C use strategies to acquire vocabulary • 1.D speak using learning strategies • 1.H develop repertoire of learning strategies • 2.E.1 use visual support to enhance understanding • 3.B.3 use routine language for classroom communication • 3.F.1 ask for information

NAME _____

WAYS TO HELP

Act it out.

Lead the way.

Write it down.

Say it another way.

Be supportive.

ELPS 1.C use strategies to acquire vocabulary • 1.D speak using learning strategies • 1.H develop repertoire of learning strategies • 2.E.1 use visual support to enhance understanding • 3.B.3 use routine language for classroom communication • 3.F.1 ask for information

Word Recognition

HIGH-FREQUENCY WORDS

 These are the most commonly used English words. Practice reading and spelling these words in order to become better readers and writers.

Unit 1	Unit 2	Unit 3	Unit 4
the	for	from	when
of	on	or	your
and	are	one	can
a	as	had	said
to	with	by	there
in	his	word	use
is	they	but	an
you	I	not	each
that	at	what	which
it	be	all	she
he	this	were	do
was	have	we	how

Unit 5	Unit 6	Unit 7	Unit 8
their	her	see	oil
if	would	number	sit
will	make	no	now
up	like	way	find
other	him	could	long
about	into	people	down
out	time	my	day
many	has	than	did
then	look	first	get
them	two	water	come
these	more	been	made
so	write	call	may
some	go	who	part

NAME —

MONITORING LISTENING CHECKLIST

	Unit 1	Unit 2	Unit 3
	Faces and Places	Crafty Creatures	Then and Now
1. What is the topic?			
2. I knew about the topic _____.	☐ already ☐ not at all	☐ already ☐ not at all	☐ already ☐ not at all
3. I knew _____ of the words.	☐ most ☐ some ☐ few	☐ most ☐ some ☐ few	☐ most ☐ some ☐ few
4. I followed _____ of my teacher's directions.	☐ most ☐ some ☐ none	☐ most ☐ some ☐ none	☐ most ☐ some ☐ none
5. I understood _____ sentences.	☐ most ☐ some ☐ few	☐ most ☐ some ☐ few	☐ most ☐ some ☐ few
6. When I didn't understand, I _____.	☐ asked for help ☐ said nothing	☐ asked for help ☐ said nothing	☐ asked for help ☐ said nothing

ELPS 2.D.1 monitor understanding of spoken language during classroom instruction and interactions • 2.D.2 seek clarification of spoken language • 2.G.1 understand general meaning: focus on topics • 2.G.2 understand general meaning: focus on language • 2.G.3 • understand general meaning: focus on contexts • 2.H.1 understand implicit ideas in increasingly complex spoken language • 2.H.2 understand information in increasingly complex spoken language • 2.I.1 demonstrate listening comprehension by following directions

9

NAME _____

CHECKLIST

Word	I've never heard of it.	I've heard of it.	I know what it means.
affect	☐	☐	☐
symbol	☐	☐	☐
trail	☐	☐	☐
celebrate	☐	☐	☐
scale	☐	☐	☐
market	☐	☐	☐

Which word did you find most challenging?

_____

NAME

CHECKLIST

Word	I've never heard of it.	I've heard of it.	I know what it means.
farming	☐	☐	☐
fishing	☐	☐	☐
population	☐	☐	☐
continent	☐	☐	☐
compass rose	☐	☐	☐
common	☐	☐	☐

Which word did you find most interesting?

_____

NAME _____

MONITORING SPEAKING CHECKLIST

	Unit 1	Unit 2	Unit 3
	"Muddy Shoes"	"Luke's Bad Day"	"The Haunted Basement"
1. When I speak in class, I usually use ____.	☐ one or two words ☐ phrases ☐ complete sentences	☐ one or two words ☐ phrases ☐ complete sentences	☐ one or two words ☐ phrases ☐ complete sentences
2. I understand instructions and can repeat them in ____.	☐ one or two words ☐ phrases ☐ complete sentences	☐ one or two words ☐ phrases ☐ complete sentences	☐ one or two words ☐ phrases ☐ complete sentences
3. If asked about a story, I can identify ____.	☐ the characters ☐ the setting ☐ the conflict or problem	☐ the characters ☐ the setting ☐ the conflict or problem	☐ the characters ☐ the setting ☐ the conflict or problem
4. I can give my opinion or ideas about a story in ____.	☐ one or two words ☐ a sentence ☐ a discussion	☐ one or two words ☐ a sentence ☐ a discussion	☐ one or two words ☐ a sentence ☐ a discussion
5. I can tell my feelings about a story in ____.	☐ one or two words ☐ a sentence ☐ a discussion	☐ one or two words ☐ a sentence ☐ a discussion	☐ one or two words ☐ a sentence ☐ a discussion

ELPS 2.1.2 demonstrate listening comprehension by retelling or summarizing spoken messages • 3.B.1 identify and describe people, places, and objects • 3.B.2 retell stories supported by pictures • 3.G.1 express opinions • 3.G.2 express ideas • 3.G.3 express feelings • 3.H.1 narrate with increasing specificity and detail • 4.G.2 demonstrate comprehension of increasingly complex English by retelling or summarizing material

NAME _____

PERSONAL NARRATIVE RUBRIC

When you write a personal narrative, check it against this rubric.
Did you do all you can to make it good?

Personal Narrative
The narrative is told in the first person, using the word *I* or *we*.
The narrative clearly describes characters, setting, and plot.
The narrative expresses the writer's feelings and thoughts.
The narrative is written so that the sequence of events is clear.
There are different kinds of sentences, and the sentences do not all start with the same word.
The grammar, spelling, and punctuation in the narrative are correct.

ELPS 1.B.2 monitor written language production and employ self-corrective techniques • 4.D use prereading supports to enhance comprehension of written text • 5.D.1 edit writing for standard grammar and usage, including subject-verb agreement • 5.D.2 edit writing for standard grammar and usage, including pronoun agreement • 5.D.3 edit writing for standard grammar and usage, including appropriate verb tenses • 5.F.1 write using a variety of grade-appropriate sentence lengths • 5.F.2 write using a variety of grade-appropriate sentence patterns • 5.F.3 write using a variety of grade-appropriate connecting words • 5.G.1 narrate with increasing specificity and detail to fulfill content area writing needs

NAME _____

SEQUENCE ORGANIZER

 You can write the events in your letter in the order they happened. This will help readers better understand what you write.

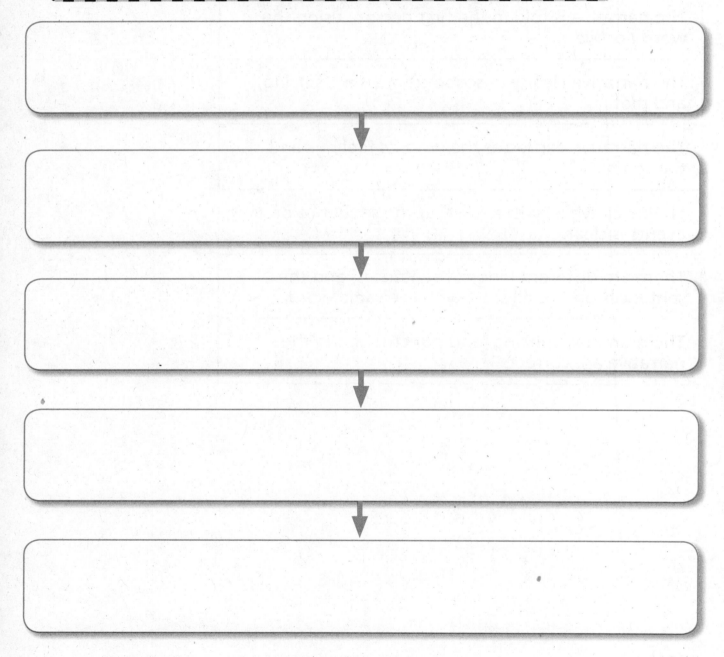

NAME _____

CAPITALIZE PROPER NOUNS

A proper noun begins with a capital letter.

A proper noun is a particular person, place, thing, or idea. *My dog's name is Bing.*

When a proper noun contains more than one word, only the important words are capitalized. *I live in the United States of America.*

People's titles are capitalized, even when they are abbreviations. *That man is Mister Smith. I saw Dr. Clark.*

An adjective that is formed from a proper noun is capitalized. *An American flag waved in the breeze.*

Rewrite each sentence. Capitalize the proper nouns.

1. jamie wrote to dr. eileen cruz.

_____

2. The panda bear has a chinese name.

_____

3. I can see venus through my telescope.

_____

4. Watch out, katie!

_____

5. The king of sweden has a crown.

_____

NAME _____

EDITING FOR GRAMMAR, SPELLING, AND PUNCTUATION

See also pages 166 and 170.

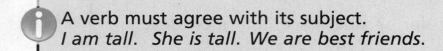

A verb must agree with its subject.
I am tall. She is tall. We are best friends.

A subject pronoun can take the place of a subject noun.

My aunt is an inventor. She builds robots.

My aunt and uncle work hard. They build amazing things.

My sister and I like robots. We like dogs, too.

A proper noun begins with a capital letter.

Listen to your teacher. Compare the first draft of a personal narrative to the edited draft.

First Draft

My mom and I visited the San Antonio Riverwalk. It (are) a path along the (san antonio river). (He) flows through the middle of the city. We walked down some steps to the river. There (is) tiny white lights hanging in all the trees. At night, (it) twinkle. We looked in several shops. Then, we stopped at a Mexican restaurant. (They) ate and watched people walk by. We had a good time!

Edited Draft

My mom and I visited the San Antonio Riverwalk. It is a path along the San Antonio River. It flows through the middle of the city. We walked down some steps to the river. There are tiny white lights hanging in all the trees. At night, they twinkle. We looked in several shops. Then, we stopped at a Mexican restaurant. We ate and watched people walk by. We had a good time!

NAME ——————————————————————————————

READER'S LOG: "HELLO!"

© HMH Supplemental Publishers Inc.

BEFORE READING: PAIR AND SHARE

1. My class talked about the

   ☐ title   ☐ illustrations   ☐ background information

2. I understood _____ of the background information.

   ☐ most or all   ☐ some   ☐ little or none

DURING READING

3. What is the main idea of the three personal narratives?

   _____

   _____

   _____

4. Is there anything in the story that you do not understand? Write about it here:

   _____

   _____

   _____

AFTER READING: PAIR AND SHARE

6. Talk to your partner about anything in the story that you do not understand.

Now, my partner and I understand . . .

Me   ☐ a lot better.   ☐ a little better.   ☐ no better.

My partner   ☐ a lot better.   ☐ a little better.   ☐ no better.

ELPS 4.E read linguistically accommodated content area material • 4.F.6 use support from peers and teachers to read content area text • 4.F.7 use support from peers and teachers to confirm understanding • 4.F.10 use support from peers and teachers to develop background knowledge

17

NAME _____

MATCH IT UP

Write the letter of the definition that matches each word.

1. _____ celebrate

   A a path that people can follow

2. _____ scale

   B something that stands for something else

3. _____ affect

   C a feature on a map that tells distances on the map

4. _____ trail

   D a place where people buy and sell things

5. _____ market

   E to do things for a special event or day

6. _____ symbol

   F to make a difference to someone or something

NAME —

WHICH WORD AM I?

Read the clues. Write the correct vocabulary word from the box to match each clue.

common	fishing	continent
farming	population	compass rose

1. I am the act of growing crops.

_____

2. I am one of the seven large land areas of the world.

_____

3. I am a sign that shows the directions north, south, east, and west on a map.

_____

4. I am the act of catching fish in the water.

_____

5. I am the number of people who live in a place.

_____

6. I am something that is seen often.

_____

NAME _____

A. What is a noun?

Read the sentences. Circle the letter of the answer that best completes the second sentence.

1. The word *girl* is a noun.
   This word names a _____.

   A person   C thing

   B place   D idea

2. The word *jar* is a noun.
   This word names a _____.

   A person   C thing

   B place   D animal

B. Subject Pronouns and *to be* verbs

Read the sentences. Circle the letter of the answer that best completes the second sentence.

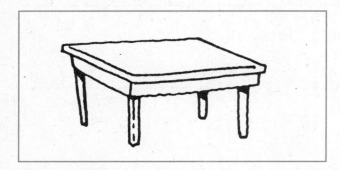

3. This is my table.
   _____ is very old.

   A She   C He

   B They   D It

4. Look at the dots.
   _____ are black.

   A They   C She

   B It   D I

ELPS 4.C.3 comprehend English vocabulary in written classroom materials • 4.C.4 comprehend English language structures in written classroom materials • 4.F.4 use visual and contextual support to develop grasp of language structures

NAME —————————————————————

5. Do you see the queen?
She _____ mad at the duck.

   A are   **C** is

   B am   **D** be

6. The dad has two kids.
They _____ all very happy.

   A are   **C** is

   B am   **D** be

PAIR AND SHARE With your partner, discuss: What is your favorite animal?

Use this sentence frame:

I like _____ the best!

Use plural nouns in your answers. Here is an example: *I like cats the best!*

Check pages 159–161 if you need help.

Monitor Language: How's your grammar?

Listen to your partner. Were the plural nouns correct?

Yes, always	Sometimes	Never
☐	☐	☐

How were your plural nouns? Were they correct?

Yes, always	Sometimes	Never
☐	☐	☐

ELPS 3.C.1 speak using a variety of grammatical structures • 3.C.2 speak using a variety of sentence lengths • 3.C.3 speak using a variety of sentence types • 4.C.3 comprehend English vocabulary in written classroom materials • 4.C.4 comprehend English language structures in written classroom materials • 4.F.4 use visual and contextual support to develop grasp of language structures • 4.F.9 use support from peers and teachers to develop language structures

NAME _____

ACTIVE READING OF THE TEXT

> **Self-monitor your understanding as you read.**
>
> 1. **Reread**. Start with the last sentence you understood. Then read on from that point.
> 2. **Take notes**. Write down the most important details. This can help you understand and remember what you read.
> 3. **Look up words you don't know.**
> 4. **Ask questions**. Then look for answers to your questions in the text, or you can ask someone.

From "Machu Picchu"	Active Reading
A trail stretches fifty miles from Cusco. It leads to Machu Picchu. This city was built by the Incas over five hundred years ago. It sits about 8,000 feet above sea level, on a mountain in the Andes. The Incas used simple tools, but they were great builders. Somehow they carried giant stones to the top of the mountain. They cut the stones to fit together exactly. About 1,000 people lived in and around Machu Picchu. The population didn't stay very long. Less than a hundred years after the Incas built the city, they left. Nobody really knows why.	Underline anything you do not understand. Take notes. What are the most important ideas? _____ _____ Tell what you reread or a question you asked. _____ _____ _____

© HMH Supplemental Publishers Inc.

ELPS 4.E read linguistically accommodated content area material • 4.G.4 demonstrate comprehension of English by taking notes

NAME ——

READ WITH EXPRESSION

Read the poem "Oranges" aloud. Read with energy and strong emotion. Pause for punctuation marks such as commas and periods. Listen to your partner's reading. Then practice the passage a second time.

Note: One slash (/) indicates a short pause for a comma. Two slashes (//) indicates that you stop for a period or a question mark.

All I wanted was a carton of juice. //

But I got mixed up, / and asked

For a crate of oranges. //

Learning a new language isn't easy. //

People notice when I get it wrong. //

But they never seem to be around

When I get it right. //

They ask me, / "Where do you come from?" //

But they never bother to ask, /

"Where are you going?" //

NAME _____

CHECK YOUR UNDERSTANDING

A. Reread "Hello!" on **Student Edition** pages 26–35. Then read each sentence below. Circle the letter of the correct answer.

Wen

1. Wen was born in _____.

A Lima

B San Antonio

C São Paolo

D Beijing

Wen

Pedro

Fernando

2. Now, Wen lives in the same city as _____.

A both Fernando and Pedro

B just Fernando

C just Pedro

D Machu Picchu

ELPS 4.E read linguistically accommodated content area material • 4.G.3 demonstrate comprehension by responding to questions

NAME —————————————————————————————

B. Read each sentence below. Circle the letter of the correct answer.

3. In Fernando's homeland, he _____.

   A helped his mother at the market

   B went to Cusco

   C spoke Portuguese

   D did a lot of fishing

4. Fernando and Pedro both _____.

   A come from the same country

   B spoke Spanish in their homeland

   C live in San Antonio now

   D came to the United States as babies

C. Read each question below. Circle the letter of the correct answer.

5. Who tells the story of each child?

   A There is no way to know who tells each story.

   B The same person tells all the stories.

   C Each child tells his or her own story.

   D Pedro tells all the stories.

6. How do you know that Wen is happy in her new city?

   A She loves going to Chinese restaurants.

   B She says she is good at English.

   C She goes to the market with her mother.

   D She has made new friends.

ELPS 4.E read linguistically accommodated content area material • 4.G.3 demonstrate comprehension by responding to questions

NAME _____

A. Label

Write a word that names each picture. Use a word from the word box.

egg	hat	jam	mop	
lip	sax	sack	duck	zip

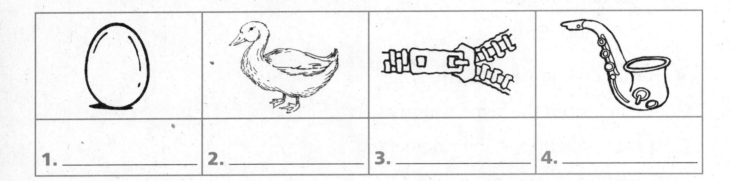

1._____ 2._____ 3._____ 4._____

B. Phonics

Read these words aloud. Use the phonics skills you have learned.

	A	B	C	D	E	F
5.	fan	Rex	it	not	up	no
6.	van	jet	quit	lot	sun	hi
7.	sat	egg	six	pop	fun	so
8.	has	yes	is	on	but	by
9.	mat	ten	zip	rock	cut	go
10.	gap	well	kill	sock	luck	my

C. High-Frequency Words

Read these words aloud.

11.	the	of	and	a	to	in
12.	is	you	that	it	he	was

ELPS 2.B recognize elements of the English sound system in newly acquired vocabulary • 3.A practice producing sounds of newly acquired vocabulary • 4.A.1 learn relationships between sounds and letters of the English language • 4.C.1 develop basic sight vocabulary • 5.A learn relationships between sounds and letters written in English • 5.C.1 spell familiar English words • 5.C.2 employ English spelling patterns • 5.C.3 employ English spelling rules

NAME —————————————————————————

D. Listen. Read. Check.

Your teacher will say a word. Mark the box next to the word.

13.	☐ me	☐ my	☐ hi
14.	☐ it	☐ hit	☐ at
15.	☐ fan	☐ fin	☐ fun
16.	☐ pit	☐ pet	☐ pot
17.	☐ sick	☐ sack	☐ sock
18.	☐ no	☐ not	☐ Nat
19.	☐ six	☐ sit	☐ sat
20.	☐ jet	☐ get	☐ Jed

E. Spelling

Your teacher will say a word. Write the word. Check your spelling.

21. _____   23. _____

22. _____   24. _____

ELPS 2.B recognize elements of the English sound system in newly acquired vocabulary • 3.A practice producing sounds of newly acquired vocabulary • 3.B.1 use high-frequency words to identify and describe people, places, and objects • 4.A.1 learn relationships between sounds and letters of the English language • 4.C.1 develop basic sight vocabulary • 5.A learn relationships between sounds and letters written in English • 5.C.1 spell familiar English words • 5.C.2 employ English spelling patterns • 5.C.3 employ English spelling rules

27

NAME _____

CHECKLIST

Word	I've never heard of it.	I've heard of it.	I know what it means.
unique	☐	☐	☐
trait	☐	☐	☐
nature	☐	☐	☐
fish	☐	☐	☐
fin	☐	☐	☐
scales	☐	☐	☐

Which word did you find most challenging?

_____

ELPS 1.C use strategic learning techniques to acquire basic and grade-level vocabulary

NAME —————————————————————————————

CHECKLIST

Word	I've never heard of it.	I've heard of it.	I know what it means.
bird	☐	☐	☐
bill	☐	☐	☐
cause	☐	☐	☐
describe	☐	☐	☐
mammal	☐	☐	☐
reptile	☐	☐	☐

Which word did you find most interesting?

_____

ELPS 1.C use strategic learning techniques to acquire basic and grade-level vocabulary

NAME _____

JOURNAL ENTRY RUBRIC

When you write a journal entry, check it against this rubric. Did you do all you can to make it good?

Journal Entry
The journal entry is personal. The writer uses the words *I* or *we*.
The writer writes the date he or she wrote the entry.
The journal entry is about an event that was important to the writer.
The writer uses descriptive language that gives a picture of the event.
The journal entry is neatly written.
The writer uses correct grammar, spelling, and punctuation.

ELPS 1.B.2 monitor written language production and employ self-corrective techniques • 4.D use prereading supports to enhance comprehension of written text • 5.D.1 edit writing for standard grammar and usage, including subject-verb agreement • 5.D.2 edit writing for standard grammar and usage, including pronoun agreement • 5.D.3 edit writing for standard grammar and usage, including appropriate verb tenses • 5.G.1 narrate with increasing specificity and detail to fulfill content area writing needs

NAME —————————————————————————————————

MAIN IDEA AND DETAILS ORGANIZER

 A journal entry starts with the date. Then, you write the main idea of the entry. After that, you list details that tell about the main idea.

Date ————————————————————————————

Main Idea

Supporting Detail

Supporting Detail

Supporting Detail

ELPS 4.D use prereading supports to enhance comprehension of written text • 5.G.1 narrate with increasing specificity and detail to fulfill content area writing needs

NAME _____

END PUNCTUATION

>  **Every sentence needs punctuation at the end.**
>
> **.**   A statement tells or describes something. A statement ends with a period.
> *The squirrel ran up the tree.*
>
> **?**   A question asks something. A question ends with a question mark.
> *Do you want to go to the park?*
>
> **!**   An exclamation expresses excitement, the need to act, or a feeling. An exclamation ends with an exclamation point.
> *I love walking in the park!*
>
> **.** or **!**   A command, or imperative, tells someone to do something. A command ends with a period or an exclamation point.
> *Open your notebooks. Don't touch that wild animal!*

Write the correct end punctuation for each sentence.

1. I'm excited about visiting the park _____

2. Where did you see the squirrel _____

3. The squirrel has a nest in the tree _____

4. What is the squirrel eating _____

5. Take a picture of the squirrel _____

6. Be quiet _____

7. You'll frighten the squirrel away _____

8. There it goes _____

NAME —————————————————————————————

EDITING FOR GRAMMAR, SPELLING, AND PUNCTUATION

See also pages 159 and 170.

 Some plural words end in *–s*. Some end in *–es*.

turtle and *turtles*   *fox* and *foxes*

 A verb must agree with its subject. Read these examples using forms of the verb *to be*.

I am here.	*I was here.*	*We are all here.*	*We were all here.*
You are here.	*You were here.*	*You are all here.*	*You were all here.*
She is here.	*She was here.*	*They are all here.*	*They were all here.*

 Every sentence ends with punctuation.

Listen to your teacher. Compare the first draft of a journal entry to the edited draft.

June 16

Something funny happened this evening. We sat outside after dinner. It (were) very dark. At first, it was quiet⋀Then, something rustled in the (bushs). Suddenly, there was a loud burping noise. Mom said it was a frog. It must have been as big as a dinner plate to make a noise that loud⋀Soon, other frogs joined in. "They (is) all around us," I said. The quiet was gone.

June 16

Something funny happened this evening. We sat outside after dinner. It was very dark. At first, it was quiet. Then, something rustled in the bushes. Suddenly, there was a loud burping noise. Mom said it was a frog. It must have been as big as a dinner plate to make a noise that loud! Soon, other frogs joined in. "They are all around us," I said. The quiet was gone.

ELPS 5.D.1 edit writing for standard grammar and usage, including subject-verb agreement • 5.E employ increasingly complex grammatical structures in content area writing

© HMH Supplemental Publishers Inc.

NAME _____

READER'S LOG: "HOW DO ANIMALS KNOW WHERE THEY ARE GOING?"

> ⓘ Active listeners take notes. Active readers do, too. Write only what you need to remember the most important information.

PAIR AND SHARE Reread the selection with your partner. Mark the boxes and take notes as you read. Add to your notes as you talk to your partner.

1. How difficult is the selection?
   ☐ very difficult ☐ not too difficult ☐ easy

2. What makes the selection difficult?
   ☐ the words ☐ the information ☐ everything!

3. List the most difficult words.

_____

4. What did you do about the difficult words?
   ☐ We talked about them. ☐ We looked at the pictures.
   ☐ We looked them up in a dictionary. ☐ We asked our teacher.

5. What did you and your partner already know?

   Me   My partner
   ☐   ☐   a lot about animals' sense of direction
   ☐   ☐   something about animals' sense of direction
   ☐   ☐   very little—the information was new

6. How did you use the pictures? Did they help you?

_____

7. Are there any sentences that you don't understand?
   Note the page number, and ask your teacher what they mean. _____

ELPS 2.I.5 demonstrate listening comprehension by taking notes • 4.E read linguistically accommodated content area material • 4.F.6 use support from peers and teachers to read content area text • 4.F.7 use support from peers and teachers to confirm understanding • 4.F.8 use support from peers and teachers to develop vocabulary • 4.F.9 use support from peers and teachers to develop language structures • 4.F.10 use support from peers and teachers to develop background knowledge • 4.G.1 demonstrate comprehension by participating in shared reading • 4.G.4 demonstrate comprehension of English by taking notes

NAME ————————————————————————————————————

UNSCRAMBLE THE WORDS

Unscramble each word to spell one of the words in the box. Write the word on the line under the scrambled word.

NATURE	FIN	UNIQUE
SCALES	FISH	TRAIT

1. ALCESS (what cover the bodies of some animals)

_____

2. RITTA (something that makes one person different from another)

_____

3. HIFS (an animal that lives in the water)

_____

4. RETANU (everything that is not made by people)

_____

5. NFI (part of a fish that helps it move)

_____

6. EQUINU (not like anything else)

_____

NAME _____

USE CLUES

Read each sentence. Use context clues to help you figure out the correct vocabulary word from the box to complete each sentence. Write the word on the line.

mammal	reptile	cause	describe	bird	bill

1. The feathers of a _____ can be many colors.

   _____

2. When I _____ my brother, I say that he is very tall.

   _____

3. Many people think a dolphin is a fish, but it is a _____.

   _____

4. The bird grabbed the worm in its _____ and ate it whole.

   _____

5. Jake thought the _____ would be slimy, but its skin was dry and rough.

   _____

6. Too much rain will _____ the river to flood.

   _____

ELPS 4.C.3 comprehend English vocabulary in written classroom materials

NAME ————————————————————————————

A. Subject Pronouns and *to be* Verbs

Circle the letter of the correct answer.

1. My sister and I work out.
We _____ strong.

   A was   **C** is

   B are   **D** were

2. Please sing more, Marissa!
_____ are a good singer!

   A He   **C** We

   B She   **D** You

3. Listen to me! Do what I say!
I _____ the king.

   A is   **C** am

   B are   **D** will

4. This is my city!
_____ is huge!

   A It   **C** We

   B She   **D** They

ELPS 4.C.3 comprehend English vocabulary in written classroom materials • 4.C.4 comprehend English language structures in written classroom materials • 4.F.4 use visual and contextual support to develop grasp of language structures

37

NAME _____

B. Combining Sentences

Write one new sentence that combines the information in the sentences above each picture.

The book is in my room.
The phone is in my room.

My dad cooks. My mom cooks.
I cook.

5. _____

6. _____

_____.

_____.

PAIR AND SHARE With your partner, discuss words you can use to describe yourselves. Use nouns and adjectives.

Use these sentence frames:

A. Nouns
   I am a _____. (brother, boy, son)
   You are a _____. (friend, student)

B. Adjectives
   I am _____. (thin, tall, tired)
   You are _____. (friendly, helpful)

Check page 164 to review adjectives. Make sure you use the correct verb form. See page 170 to review forms of *to be*.

Monitor Language: How's your grammar?

Listen to your partner. Were the nouns, adjectives, and verb forms correct?

Yes, always	Sometimes	Never
☐	☐	☐

How were your nouns, adjectives, and verb forms? Were they correct?

Yes, always	Sometimes	Never
☐	☐	☐

ELPS 3.B.1 use high-frequency words to identify and describe people, places, and objects • 3.C.1 speak using a variety of grammatical structures • 3.C.2 speak using a variety of sentence lengths • 3.C.3 speak using a variety of sentence types • 4.C.3 comprehend English vocabulary in written classroom materials • 4.C.4 comprehend English language structures in written classroom materials • 4.F.4 use visual and contextual support to develop grasp of language structures • 4.F.9 use support from peers and teachers to develop language structures

NAME —————————————————————————

ACTIVE READING OF THE TEXT

 Self-monitor your understanding as you read.

1. **Reread**. Start with the last sentence you understood. Then read on from that point.

2. **Take notes**. Write down the most important details. This can help you understand and remember what you read.

3. **Look up words you don't know.**

4. **Ask questions**. Then look for answers to your questions in the text, or you can ask someone.

From "Gus Helps Huck Get Honey"	Active Reading
Huck is a honey badger. He lives in the grasslands in East Africa. Just like all honey badgers, Huck is tough. He is a fierce hunter. There are plenty of animals that Huck hunts. He is a snake killer. He can eat a five-foot snake in fifteen minutes. Scales and all! Huck also eats insects, reptiles, and small mammals. What he loves most of all, though, is honey. Honey isn't always that easy to find. That's why it's a good thing that Huck has a friend called Gus.	Underline anything you do not understand. Take notes. What are the most important ideas? ——————————————— ——————————————— ——————————————— Tell what you reread or a question you asked. ——————————————— ——————————————— ———————————————

NAME _____

READ FOR RATE

Read "How to Build a Trap" aloud. Have a partner time your reading for one minute. Then, fill in the chart at the bottom of the page with the number of words you read. Read the passage a second and third time. Try to increase the number of words you read accurately in a minute.

A spider web stretches between two objects. They may be	10
branches of a tree, or even the legs of a chair.	21
First, the spider spins a thin thread. The thread is carried by	33
the tiniest breeze. It makes a line between the two objects.	44
The spider makes threads from the center. Now you could	54
describe the web as looking like a bicycle wheel. Next, the	65
spider makes sticky threads in circles.	71
It's done, and the spider waits. An insect lands on the web.	83
It gets stuck. The spider rushes up! It bites! It wraps the insect	96
with more thread.	99
Dinner is served.	102

Number of Words Read		
First Reading	Second Reading	Third Reading

NAME _____

CHECK YOUR UNDERSTANDING

A. Reread "How Do Animals Know Where They Are Going?" on **Student Edition** pages 72–81. Then read each sentence. Circle the letter of the correct answer.

how animals find their way

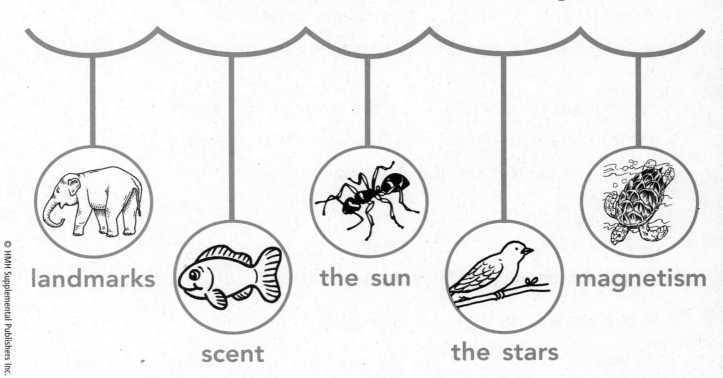

landmarks   scent   the sun   the stars   magnetism

1. Salmon find their way by using _____.

   A the sun   **C** landmarks

   B scent   **D** the stars

2. Animals that use landmarks include _____.

   A elephants   **C** bats

   B bees   **D** loggerhead turtles

ELPS 4.E read linguistically accommodated content area material • 4.G.3 demonstrate comprehension by responding to questions

41

NAME _____

B. Read each sentence below. Circle the letter of the correct answer.

3. One animal that travels by night is _____ .

    A the ant   **C** the wildebeest

    B the indigo bunting   **D** the elephant

4. The selection tells how _____ use magnetism.

    A wildebeests   **C** ants and some birds

    B most insects   **D** bats and some turtles

C. Read each question below. Circle the letter of the correct answer.

5. Which fact about ants is <u>most</u> important to the selection?

    A The sun helps them find their way.

    B They live in nests.

    C They travel in a straight line.

    D They sometimes go far from their nests.

6. Which animals do NOT use magnetism to find their way?

    A bats

    B salmon

    C loggerhead turtles

    D humans

ELPS 4.E read linguistically accommodated content area material • 4.G.3 demonstrate comprehension by responding to questions

NAME —

A. Label

Write a word that names each picture. Use a word from the box.

bat	cub	boat	cube	ran	kit	rain	kite

1. _____	2. _____	3. _____	4. _____

B. Phonics

Read these words aloud. Use the phonics skills you have learned.

	A	B	C	D	E	F	G
5.	see	pane	kite	may	home	Eve	fume
6.	rain	tame	line	team	lone	Zeke	cube
7.	pay	safe	mile	coat	doze	Pete	tube
8.	toad	quake	pipe	keep	mole	beet	mute
9.	meat	tape	bite	pain	bone	peek	tune
10.	be	wade	hike	say	cope	feat	rude

C. High-Frequency Words

Read these words aloud.

11.	for	on	are	as	with	his
12.	they	I	at	be	this	have

© HMH Supplemental Publishers Inc.

ELPS 2.B recognize elements of the English sound system in newly acquired vocabulary • 3.A practice producing sounds of newly acquired vocabulary • 4.A.1 learn relationships between sounds and letters of the English language • 4.C.1 develop basic sight vocabulary • 5.A learn relationships between sounds and letters when writing in Pnglish • 5.C.1 spell familiar English words • 5.C.2 employ English spelling pattern • 5.C.3 employ English spelling rules

NAME _____

D. Listen. Read. Check.

Your teacher will say a word. Mark the box next to the word.

13.	☐ quake	☐ cake	☐ quack
14.	☐ way	☐ wade	☐ wait
15.	☐ rain	☐ ray	☐ ran
16.	☐ cub	☐ cube	☐ cab
17.	☐ bit	☐ by	☐ bite
18.	☐ mutt	☐ mute	☐ muck
19.	☐ feed	☐ fed	☐ feet
20.	☐ pat	☐ pet	☐ Pete

E. Spelling

Your teacher will say a word. Write the word. Check your spelling.

21. _____   23. _____

22. _____   24. _____

© HMH Supplemental Publishers Inc.

ELPS 2.B recognize elements of the English sound system in newly acquired vocabulary • 3.A practice producing sounds of newly acquired vocabulary • 4.A.1 learn relationships between sounds and letters of the English language • 4.C.1 develop basic sight vocabulary • 5.A learn relationships between sounds and letters when writing in English • 5.C.1 spell familiar English words • 5.C.2 employ English spelling pattern • 5.C.3 employ English spelling rules

NAME ———————————————————————

CHECKLIST

Word	I've never heard of it.	I've heard of it.	I know what it means.
travel	☐	☐	☐
past	☐	☐	☐
present	☐	☐	☐
transportation	☐	☐	☐
railroad	☐	☐	☐
possible	☐	☐	☐

Which word did you find most challenging?

———————————————————————

ELPS 1.C use strategic learning techniques to acquire basic and grade-level vocabulary.

45

NAME _____

CHECKLIST

Word	I've never heard of it.	I've heard of it.	I know what it means.
modern	☐	☐	☐
assembly line	☐	☐	☐
advanced	☐	☐	☐
century	☐	☐	☐
decade	☐	☐	☐
purpose	☐	☐	☐

Which word did you find most interesting?

_____

NAME _____

READING LONGER WORDS

 Reading Closed Syllables When a word or syllable has one vowel and ends in a consonant, the vowel usually stands for a *short* vowel sound.

 You can divide:

- between the words in a compound word.
- after a prefix, or before a suffix.
- between the consonants in a VCCV letter pattern.

A. Draw a slash (/) between the two words. Read the smaller words. Then read the compound word.

c a n n o t	s u n s e t	b a c k p a c k

B. Draw a slash (/) between the two word parts. Read the word parts. Then read the compound word.

u n l i t	u n p a c k	d i s m i s s

C. In longer words, look for a VCCV letter pattern (a vowel plus two consonants plus another vowel).

u p s e t	n a p k i n	f a b r i c

D. Use the strategies you have learned to divide the words. Read each part. Then read the whole word.

c a c t u s	p a d l o c k	p u b l i c

NAME _____

FRIENDLY LETTER RUBRIC

When you write a friendly letter, compare it to this rubric. Did you do all you can to make it good?

Friendly Letter
The letter is in the first person, using the word *I* or *we*.
The letter has the date, a greeting, a body, and a closing.
The letter is written to communicate with a friend.
The letter expresses the writer's feelings and thoughts.
The letter is readable and clearly written.
There are different kinds of sentences, and the sentences do not all start with the same word.
The grammar, spelling, and punctuation in the letter are correct.

ELPS 1.B.2 monitor written language production and employ self-corrective techniques • 4.D use prereading supports to enhance comprehension of written text • 5.D.1 edit writing for standard grammar and usage, including subject-verb agreement • 5.D.2 edit writing for standard grammar and usage, including pronoun agreement • 5.D.3 edit writing for standard grammar and usage, including appropriate verb tenses • 5.F.1 write using a variety of grade-appropriate sentence lengths • 5.F.2 write using a variety of grade-appropriate sentence patterns • 5.F.3 write using a variety of grade-appropriate connecting words • 5.G.1 narrate with increasing specificity and detail to fulfill content area writing needs

NAME —————————————————————————————

CAUSE AND EFFECT ORGANIZER

An **event** is something that happens.

A **cause** makes something happen.

An **effect** is what happens.

You can organize writing to describe the cause and effects of an event. First, write a few words to tell what event you will write about. Then, describe the cause. What made the event happen? Next, describe the effects. What happened as a result of the cause?

Event ——————————————————————————————

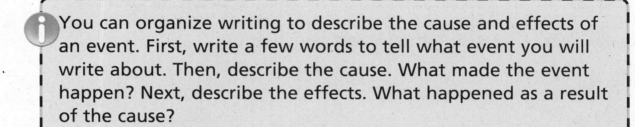

Cause

Effect

Effect

© HMH Supplemental Publishers Inc.

NAME _____

USE COMMAS IN A LIST

 Commas tell a reader where to pause. We use commas to separate three or more items in a list.

Bicycles, roller skates, and skateboards have wheels.
She got on her bike, pedaled hard, and flew down
the street.

Rewrite each sentence, using the correct punctuation.

1. Maria Tran and Luis went to the park.

_____

2. The park has trails a lake and rides.

_____

3. Children adults and pets walked on the trails.

_____

4. People swam fished and watched ducks at the lake.

_____

5. Tran carried a blanket a picnic basket and a book.

_____

6. Maria carried water cups and plates.

_____

7. Luis brought napkins forks and spoons.

_____

8. They ate sandwiches and fruit.

_____

NAME _____

EDITING FOR GRAMMAR, SPELLING, AND PUNCTUATION

See also pages 173 and 174.

 The present tense of a verb describes an action that is happening now. *The horses walk down the street.*

 The past tense of a verb describes action that happened in the past. *The horses walked down the street.*

 An adverb often describes a verb. It usually ends in *–ly.*
Incorrect: *The drums beat loud.*
Correct: *The drums beat loudly.*

Listen to your teacher. Compare the first draft of a friendly letter to the edited draft.

Dear Lydia,   September 5, 2011
    We had a terrible storm last night! I was at my cousin Sara's house. Lightning struck. A flash of light filled the room. Thunder boom. I was terrified! The wind blew fierce. It broke tree branches∧ blew leaves∧ and tore down signs. Then, the rain came. It drummed on the roof. It rattled the windows. Finally, the storm pass. We hugged each other when it was over.
                                                Your friend,
                                                Amy

Dear Lydia,   September 5, 2011
    We had a terrible storm last night! I was at my cousin Sara's house. Lightning struck. A flash of light filled the room. Thunder boomed. I was terrified! The wind blew fiercely. It broke tree branches, blew leaves, and tore down signs. Then, the rain came. It drummed on the roof. It rattled the windows. Finally, the storm passed. We hugged each other when it was over.
                                                Your friend,
                                                Amy

© HMH Supplemental Publishers Inc.

ELPS 5.D.3 edit writing for standard grammar and usage, including appropriate verb tenses • 5.E employ increasingly complex grammatical structures in content area writing

51

NAME _____

READER'S LOG: "HOW WILL WE GET TO SCHOOL TODAY?"

BEFORE READING: PAIR AND SHARE

1. My class talked about the _____.

   ☐ title   ☐ illustrations   ☐ background information

2. I understood _____ of the background information.

   ☐ most or all   ☐ some   ☐ little or none

DURING READING

3. Which character is more serious? Explain.

   _____

   _____

   _____

4. Is there anything in the story that you do not understand? Write about it here:

   _____

   _____

AFTER READING: PAIR AND SHARE

5. Talk to your partner about anything that you did not understand.

Now, my partner and I understand _____.

Me   ☐ a lot better   ☐ a little better   ☐ no better

My partner   ☐ a lot better   ☐ a little better   ☐ no better

ELPS 4.E read linguistically accommodated content area material • 4.F.6 use support from peers and teachers to read content area text • 4.F.7 use support from peers and teachers to confirm understanding • 4.F.10 use support from peers and teachers to develop background knowledge • 4.G.1 demonstrate comprehension by participating in shared reading

NAME ——————————————————————————————

WHICH WORD?

Write the vocabulary word from the box to complete each sentence.

| present | railroad | travel |
| possible | past | transportation |

1. When people ——, they go from place to place.

——————————————————————————————

2. Something that happened long ago happened in the ——.

——————————————————————————————

3. If something is ——, you can do it.

——————————————————————————————

4. Railroads, cars, and airplanes are different kinds of ——.

——————————————————————————————

5. Trains travel along the steel tracks of a ——.

——————————————————————————————

6. Something that is happening in the —— is happening now.

——————————————————————————————

NAME _____

MATCH IT UP

Write the letter of the definition that matches each word.

1. ___ century

    A part of a factory where work passes from one person to the next

2. ___ purpose

    B ten years

3. ___ assembly line

    C the reason that something exists

4. ___ decade

    D something new and from the present

5. ___ advanced

    E one hundred years

6. ___ modern

    F greatly developed and using new ideas

NAME —————————————————————————

A. Action Verbs: Present Tense
Circle the letter of the correct answer.

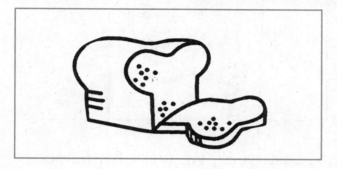

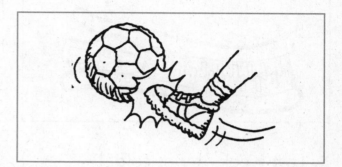

1. I like bread a lot. Juan _____ it a lot, too.

   A like   **C** liking

   B likes   **D** liked

2. Dan kicks the ball. Marta kicks the ball. We all _____ the ball.

   A kicks   **C** kick

   B licking   **D** were

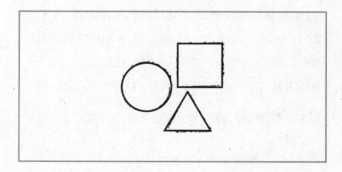

3. Look at the ducks! They _____ all the time.

   A quack   **C** quacking

   B quacks   **D** are

4. I see the shapes. Kim _____ the shapes too.

   A sees   **C** seeing

   B see   **D** is

ELPS 4.C.1 develop basic sight vocabulary • 4.C.4 comprehend English language structures used in written classroom materials • 4.F.4 use visual and contextual support to develop grasp of language structures

55

NAME _____

B. Action Verbs: Past Tense

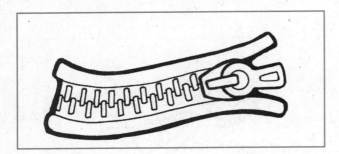

5. Last week, it was cold. I _____ up my coat to the top.

   A zip   **C** zipped

   B zipping   **D** zipper

6. Last week, we went to the zoo. Roberto _____ all day.

   A smiles   **C** smiling

   B smiled   **D** will smile

PAIR AND SHARE With your partner, discuss how you spend your weekends. What action verbs can you use to describe what you do? Ask your partner questions about her or his activities.

Use these sentence frames:

A. Tell about yourself.

On the weekend, I usually _____. (run, play, study, sleep)

B. Tell about what a family member or friend does on weekends.

On the weekend, my dad usually _____. (plays chess, watches TV, reads books)

Check page 173 to review action verbs. Make sure you use the correct verb form.

Monitor Language: How's your grammar?

Listen to your partner. Were the verb forms correct?

Yes, always	Sometimes	Never
☐	☐	☐

How were your verb forms? Were they correct?

Yes, always	Sometimes	Never
☐	☐	☐

ELPS 3.C.1 speak using a variety of grammatical structures • 3.C.2 speak using a variety of sentence lengths • 3.C.3 speak using a variety of sentence types • 4.C.1 develop basic sight vocabulary • 4.C.4 comprehend English language structures used in written classroom materials • 4.F.4 use visual and contextual support to develop grasp of language structures • 4.F.9 use support from peers and teachers to develop language structures

NAME ——————————————————————————————————

ACTIVE READING OF THE TEXT

 Self-monitor your understanding as you read.

1. **Reread**. Start with the last sentence you understood. Then read on from that point.

2. **Take notes**. Write down the most important details. This can help you understand and remember what you read.

3. **Look up words you don't know.**

4. **Ask questions**. Then look for answers to your questions in the text, or you can ask someone.

From "The Transportation Century"	Active Reading
Transportation changed in the twentieth century.	Underline anything you do not understand.
In 1900, people depended on horses. Some cities had electric streetcars. Many buses were pulled by horses.	Take notes. What are the most important ideas?
People traveled by train between cities. In the country, there weren't many ways to get around. There were only 9,000 cars on the road. And there weren't very many roads!	Tell what you reread or a question you asked.
A lot happened in the first decade of the century. The airplane was invented. The first car that people could afford was made. Things were beginning to change.	

NAME _____

READ FOR ACCURACY

Work with a partner. Take turns reading the passage aloud. Try to speak clearly and pronounce each word correctly. Then review the passage together. Write the difficult words on the lines below. Practice saying the words aloud. Then read the passage a second time.

> You can be glad you didn't have to ride the first kind of bike. It had wooden wheels and iron tires. It was called "the boneshaker."
>
> Next came a bicycle with rubber tires. It was much more popular!
>
> Today's bicycles are light and fast. They have gears. This helps the rider get the most out of the bike.
>
> Bikes don't need any fuel. Riding a bike is kind to the planet, and good for your health.

© HMH Supplemental Publishers Inc.

_____   _____

_____   _____

_____   _____

_____   _____

_____   _____

NAME _____

CHECK YOUR UNDERSTANDING

A. Read the following questions about "The Transportation Century" on **Student Edition** pages 128–133. Circle the letter of the correct answer.

1900	1950	2000

first airplane   first space shuttle

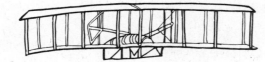

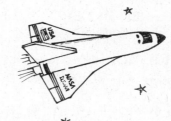

1. People started flying in airplanes _____.

   A before 1900   **C** in 1950

   B before 1910   **D** after 1950

2. The space shuttle was invented _____.

   A before the airplane   **C** after 1950

   B before 1950   **D** after 2000

ELPS 4.E read linguistically accommodated content area material • 4.G.3 demonstrate comprehension by responding to questions

59

NAME _____

B. Read each sentence below. Circle the letter of the
   correct answer.

3. The twentieth century began in the year _____.

   A 2000   **C** 1920

   B 1900   **D** 1999

4. The first city buses were _____.

   A electric   **C** invented after the airplane

   B the same size as cars   **D** pulled by horses

C. Read each question below. Circle the letter of the
   correct answer.

5. How did transportation change from 1910 to 1950?

   A Millions more cars were on the road by 1950.

   B There were no more trains by 1950.

   C The space shuttle started flying between cities.

   D There were 9,000 cars in 1950.

6. What does the selection tell about jetpacks?

   A Jetpacks were a new invention in 2000.

   B Travelers get around by jetpack all the time now.

   C Travelers may use jetpacks someday.

   D People traveled to the moon and back with jetpacks.

NAME —————————————————————

A. Label

Write a word that names each picture. Use a word from the word box.

pad	page	ship	chip	bath	shapes
		cent	sell		

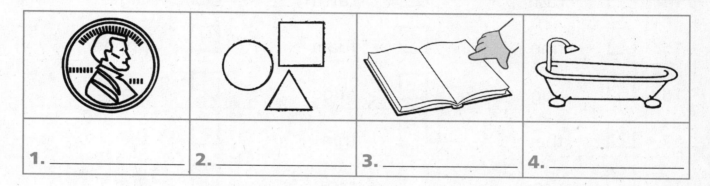

1. _____
2. _____
3. _____
4. _____

B. Phonics

Read these words aloud. Use the phonics skills you have learned.

	A	B	C	D	E	F	G
5.	ship	sheet	path	thus	ace	game	gem
6.	chip	leash	thin	then	cage	coal	cell
7.	cash	wheel	math	that	mice	goal	gel
8.	rich	phone	with	them	huge	cope	cent
9.	rash	whee	thick	than	race	gain	gene
10.	catch	cheap	bath	this	wage	cone	cease

C. High-Frequency Words

Read these words aloud.

11.	from	or	one	had	by	word
12.	but	not	what	all	were	we

ELPS 2.B recognize elements of the English sound system in newly acquired vocabulary • 3.A practice producing sounds of newly acquired vocabulary • 4.A.1 learn relationships between sounds and letters of the English language • 4.C.1 develop basic sight vocabulary • 5.A learn relationships between sounds and letters written in English • 5.C.1 spell familiar English words • 5.C.2 employ English spelling patterns • 5.C.3 employ English spelling rules

NAME _____

D. Listen. Read. Check.

Your teacher will say a word. Mark the box next to the word.

13.	☐ rash	☐ rich	☐ chip
14.	☐ cash	☐ catch	☐ cage
15.	☐ fine	☐ foam	☐ phone
16.	☐ hug	☐ huge	☐ jug
17.	☐ the	☐ thin	☐ them
18.	☐ rice	☐ race	☐ Russ
19.	☐ whip	☐ wipe	☐ hip
20.	☐ age	☐ jay	☐ gem

E. Spelling

Your teacher will say a word. Write the word. Check your spelling.

21. _____   23. _____

22. _____   24. _____

ELPS 2.B recognize elements of the English sound system in newly acquired vocabulary • 3.A practice producing sounds of newly acquired vocabulary • 4.A.1 learn relationships between sounds and letters of the English language • 4.C.1 develop basic sight vocabulary • 5.A learn relationships between sounds and letters written in English • 5.C.1 spell familiar English words • 5.C.2 employ English spelling patterns • 5.C.3 employ English spelling rules

NAME —————————————————————————————————

MONITORING LISTENING CHECKLIST

> ℹ Active listeners take notes. Don't try to write everything. Just note what you need in order to remember the most important information.

	Unit 4 Making Life Easier	Unit 5 Shoot for the Stars	Unit 6 Our Valuable Earth
1. What is the topic?			
2. The general meaning of the discussion was _____.			
3. I knew most of the words _____.	☐ already ☐ not at all	☐ very familiar ☐ unfamiliar	☐ very familiar ☐ unfamiliar
4. I understood the sentences _____.	☐ most of the time ☐ sometimes ☐ almost never	☐ most of the time ☐ sometimes ☐ almost never	☐ most of the time ☐ sometimes ☐ almost never
5. The main point of this topic is now _____.	☐ very clear ☐ a little clearer ☐ still confusing	☐ very clear ☐ a little clearer ☐ still confusing	☐ very clear ☐ a little clearer ☐ still confusing
6. My notes helped me understand the discussion _____.	☐ a lot ☐ a little ☐ not at all	☐ a lot ☐ a little ☐ not at all	☐ a lot ☐ a little ☐ not at all

ELPS 2.G.4 understand main points of topics • 2.G.5 understand main points language • 2.G.6 understand main points of contexts • 2.H.1 understand implicit ideas • 2.H.2 understand information • 2.I.2 demonstrate listening comprehension by retelling or summarizing spoken messages • 2.I.5 demonstrate listening comprehension by taking notes

NAME _____

CHECKLIST

Word	I've never heard of it.	I've heard of it.	I know what it means.
calculator	☐	☐	☐
monitor	☐	☐	☐
keyboard	☐	☐	☐
computer	☐	☐	☐
printer	☐	☐	☐
type	☐	☐	☐

Which word did you find most challenging?

_____

NAME ——————————————————————————————

CHECKLIST

Word	I've never heard of it.	I've heard of it.	I know what it means.
robot	☐	☐	☐
chore	☐	☐	☐
command	☐	☐	☐
plan	☐	☐	☐
report	☐	☐	☐
electricity	☐	☐	☐

Which word did you find most interesting?

——————————————————————————————————————

ELPS 1.C use strategic learning techniques to acquire basic and grade-level vocabulary.

NAME _____

MONITORING SPEAKING CHECKLIST

	Unit 4 "Lost Dog"	Unit 5 "Cooking Dinner"	Unit 6 "Pablo and Pedro"
1. I can describe the characters and setting in _____.	☐ one or two words ☐ phrases ☐ complete sentences	☐ one or two words ☐ phrases ☐ complete sentences	☐ one or two words ☐ phrases ☐ complete sentences
2. I can retell the story in _____.	☐ a complete way ☐ a sentence ☐ a word or two	☐ a complete way ☐ a sentence ☐ a word or two	☐ a complete way ☐ a sentence ☐ a word or two
3. I explain my opinion about the story and ideas in a way that others _____.	☐ often agree with ☐ understand ☐ do not understand	☐ often agree with ☐ understand ☐ do not understand	☐ often agree with ☐ understand ☐ do not understand
4. My speaking skills are _____.	☐ improving ☐ staying the same	☐ improving ☐ staying the same	☐ improving ☐ staying the same

ELPS 2.I.2 demonstrate listening comprehension by retelling or summarizing spoken messages • 3.B.1 use high-frequency words to identify and describe people, places, and objects • 3.B.2 retell simple stories and basic information represented or supported by pictures • 3.G.1 express opinions • 3.G.2 express ideas • 3.H.1 narrate with increasing specificity and detail • 3.H.2 describe with increasing specificity and detail • 3.H.3 explain with increasing specificity and detail

NAME _____

READING LONGER WORDS

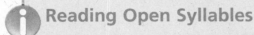

> **Reading Open Syllables**
>
> When a word or syllable ends in a vowel, the vowel usually stands for a *long* vowel sound.

> When you see a VCV letter pattern, first try dividing the word before the consonant. Read the word using a long vowel sound for the open syllable. (Example: p h o / t o) If the word doesn't sound quite right, try dividing after the consonant. Then read the word again, using a short vowel sound. (Example: p a n / i c)

A. Divide the word *before* the consonant in the VCV letter pattern. Read each syllable. Then read the whole word.

photo	ego	logo	pupil

B. Divide the word. Find the VCV letter pattern. Read each syllable. Then read the whole word.

begin	robot	cubic	music

C. Divide the word. Find the VCV letter pattern. Read each syllable. Then read the whole word.

panic	comic	rapid	robin

D. Divide the word. Find the VCV letter pattern. Read each syllable. Then read the whole word.

siren	recess	denim	humid
comet	finish	open	visit

ELPS 4.A.1 learn relationships between sounds and letters of the English language • 4.A.2 decode words using a combination of skills

NAME _____

PROCEDURAL TEXT RUBRIC

When you write a procedural, check it against this rubric. Did you do all you can to make it good?

Observation Log
A title describes the project or activity.
There is a list of necessary materials.
The procedural is told using the words you or your.
The procedural orders the steps in the process.
Each step is written clearly.
There are words that make the order of the steps clear.
The procedural is neat and easy to read.
The grammar, spelling, and punctuation in the procedural are correct.

ELPS 1.B.2 monitor written language production and employ self-corrective techniques • 4.D use prereading supports to enhance comprehension of written text • 5.D.1 edit writing for standard grammar and usage, including subject-verb agreement • 5.D.2 edit writing for standard grammar and usage, including pronoun agreement • 5.D.3 edit writing for standard grammar and usage, including appropriate verb tenses • 5.G.3 explain with increasing specificity and detail to fulfill content area writing needs

NAME —————————————————————————

STEPS IN A PROCESS ORGANIZER

 There are always steps in a process. The steps are written in order. Steps often begin with a word such as *first, second, third, next, then,* or *finally*. Write the name of the process and the materials needed. Then write the steps in order.

Title: ———————————————————————————

Materials: ———————————————————————

First, ———————————————————————————

————————————————————————————

Second, ——————————————————————————

————————————————————————————

Then, ————————————————————————————

————————————————————————————

Finally, ———————————————————————————

————————————————————————————

© HMH Supplemental Publishers Inc.

ELPS 4.D use prereading supports to enhance comprehension of written text • 5.G.3 explain with increasing specificity and detail to fulfill content area writing needs

69

NAME _____

END PUNCTUATION

> **Every sentence needs punctuation at the end.**
>
> **.**   A statement tells something or describes something. A statement ends with a period.
> *My cat is called Buster.*
>
> **?**   A question is a sentence that asks something. A question ends with a question mark.
> *Where do you live?*
>
> **!**   An exclamation is a sentence full of excitement, urgency, or feeling. An exclamation ends with an exclamation point.
> *I am so happy!*
>
> **.** or **!**   A command, or imperative, tells someone to do something. A command ends with a period or an exclamation point.
> *Stay away from that dog! Come to my house tomorrow.*

Add the correct punctuation at the end of each sentence.

1. I need to write a letter to my aunt_____

2. How much does a stamp cost_____

3. Get the mail from the mailbox_____

4. Quick, the mail truck is coming_____

5. Find the zip code_____

6. A zip code helps the post office_____

7. I love colored envelopes_____

8. Let's be pen pals_____

NAME —

EDITING FOR GRAMMAR, SPELLING, AND PUNCTUATION

See also pages 170–172.

A contraction is two words put together to make one word. An apostrophe takes the place of the missing letter or letters.

I am ⇒ I'm   you are ⇒ you're
she is ⇒ she's   he is ⇒ he's   it is ⇒ it's
we are ⇒ we're   they are ⇒ they're

A negative contraction combines a verb with the word *not*.

is not ⇒ isn't   are not ⇒ aren't
was not ⇒ wasn't   were not ⇒ weren't
does not ⇒ doesn't will not ⇒ won't

Listen to your teacher. Compare the first draft of a procedural to the edited draft.

Make Your Own Card

Have you ever made your own card It isnt hard. You need paper, scissors, glitter, magazines, glue, and markers. First, fold a piece of paper in half. Next, cut out some magazine pictures. Be sure to cut neat. Glue them to the front of the card. Add glitter. Then, write a message inside. Youre done!

Make Your Own Card

Have you ever made your own card? It isn't hard. You need paper, scissors, glitter, magazines, glue, and markers. First, fold a piece of paper in half. Next, cut out some magazine pictures. Be sure to cut neatly. Glue them to the front of the card. Add glitter. Then, write a message inside. You're done!

NAME _____

READER'S LOG: "ROBERT THE ROBOT"

BEFORE READING: PAIR AND SHARE

1. My class talked about
   ☐ titles.　　☐ illustrations.　　☐ background information.

2. I understood _____ of the background information.
   ☐ most or all　　☐ some　　☐ little or none

DURING READING

3. What are the main events in the story?

   _____

   _____

   _____

4. Is there anything in the story that you do not understand? Write it here:

   _____

   _____

   _____

AFTER READING: PAIR AND SHARE

5. Talk to your partner about anything that you did not understand.
   Now, my partner and I understand _____.
   Me　　　　　☐ a lot better　☐ a little better　☐ no better
   My partner　☐ a lot better　☐ a little better　☐ no better

ELPS 4.E read linguistically accommodated content area material • 4.F.6 use support from peers and teachers to read content area text • 4.F.7 use support from peers and teachers to confirm understanding • 4.F.10 use support from peers and teachers to develop background knowledge • 4.G.1 demonstrate comprehension by participating in shared reading

NAME _____

USE CLUES

Read each sentence. Use context clues to help you figure out the correct vocabulary word from the box to complete each sentence. Write the word on the line.

| monitor | computer | type | printer |
| keyboard | calculator |

1. A powerful _____ can do much more than emails and games.

_____

2. I have a color _____ that makes beautiful copies of drawings that I make on the computer.

_____

3. A _____ makes it easy for me to add a lot of numbers.

_____

4. Maria opened the file and looked at it on the _____ of her computer.

_____

5. Some people can _____ faster than they can write with a pencil or pen.

_____

6. The _____ of my computer has keys to type letters and keys for commands.

_____

NAME _____

UNSCRAMBLE THE WORDS

Unscramble each word to spell one of the words in the box. Write the word on the line under the scrambled word.

CHORE	PLAN	REPORT	ROBOT
	COMMAND	ELECTRICITY	

1. NAMDOCM (an order to do something)

_____

2. TREPOR (facts and ideas about a topic)

_____

3. BOORT (a machine that can help people work)

_____

4. HECOR (a job that needs to be done often)

_____

5. TETYLCRICEI (power that travels along wires)

_____

6. LANP (a drawing that shows how something is put together)

_____

NAME

Using Contractions with *to be* and *not*

Read each question. Circle the letter of the sentence that answers it.

1. Is that Dad's box?

  A Yes, it's his box.

  B Yes, they are.

  C Yes, we can.

2. Is that a drum?

  A Yes, it's a drum.

  B No, it isn't a drum.

  C It wasn't fun.

3. Are the kids pals?

  A No, it isn't.

  B He is a pal.

  C Yes, they're pals.

4. Are you kids all on the bus?

  A Yes, we're on it.

  B No, I'm not.

  C No, he isn't.

5. Is that a bell?

  A No, it isn't.

  B Yes, it's a bell.

  C You're a bell.

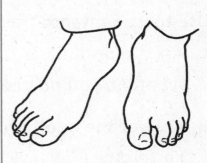

6. Were your feet sore?

  A Yes, they're feet.

  B No, I'm not.

  C Yes, they're sore.

ELPS 4.C.3 comprehend English vocabulary in written classroom materials • 4.C.4 comprehend English language structures in written classroom materials • 4.F.4 use visual and contextual support to develop grasp of language structures

75

NAME _____

7. Is it raining?

  A No, it isn't raining.

  B Yes, it's raining.

  C We're not wet.

8. Is that a fish?

  A No, I'm not.

  B Yes, it's a fish.

  C No, it isn't a fish.

PAIR AND SHARE With your partner, discuss what you did yesterday.

Use these sentence frames:

A. Ask a question.

What did you do yesterday?

B. Answer the question.

Yesterday, I _____. (cleaned my room, watched TV, finished my math)

Check page 174 to review the past tense forms of action verbs. Make sure you use the correct verb form.

Monitor Language: How's your grammar?

Listen to your partner. Were the past tense verb forms correct?

Yes, always	Sometimes	Never
☐	☐	☐

How were your verb forms? Were they correct?

Yes, always	Sometimes	Never
☐	☐	☐

© HMH Supplemental Publishers Inc.

ELPS 3.C.1 speak using a variety of grammatical structures • 3.C.2 speak using a variety of sentence lengths • 3.C.3 speak using a variety of sentence types • 4.C.3 comprehend English vocabulary in written classroom materials • 4.C.4 comprehend English language structures in written classroom materials • 4.F.4 use visual and contextual support to develop grasp of language structures • 4.F.9 use support from peers and teachers to develop grasp of language structures

NAME —————————————————————————

ACTIVE READING OF THE TEXT

 Self-monitor your understanding as you read.

1. **Reread.** Start with the last sentence you understood. Then read on from that point.

2. **Take notes.** Write down the most important details. This can help you understand and remember what you read.

3. **Look up words you don't know.**

4. **Ask questions.** Then look for answers to your questions in the text, or you can ask someone.

From "Words on Paper"	Active Reading
Some people don't have good handwriting! Luckily, the typewriter was invented. The words are always neat. Also, people can type faster than they can write. Typewriters were used all around the world for about a hundred years. Then a machine that was faster and more useful took over. The world turned to the computer. A computer lets you correct your work as you write. If you're fixing a long report, you don't have to start all over again. There are commands on the keyboard for all sorts of helpful tasks.	Underline anything you do not understand. Take notes. What are the most important ideas? _____ _____ _____ Tell what you reread or a question you asked. _____ _____ _____

ELPS 4.E read linguistically accommodated content area material • 4.G.4 demonstrate comprehension of English by taking notes

77

NAME _____

READ WITH EXPRESSION

Read aloud the following section from "Useful Stuff: The Knife." Read with energy and strong emotion. Pause for punctuation marks such as commas and periods. Listen to your partner's reading. Then practice the passage a second time.

Note: One slash (/) indicates a short pause for a comma. Two slashes (//) indicates that you stop for a period or a question mark.

> Rosa opened her lunchbox. //
> As usual, / there was a cheese sandwich. // As usual, / her mother hadn't cut the sandwich in half. // So, / as usual, / Rosa would make a mess when she ate it. //
> "Why won't Mom use a knife?" // Rosa said. // "Even cavemen used knives. // They made them by banging stones until some flaked off. // A sharp edge was left." //
> "You can use this plastic knife," / said Elva. // "But it won't be much good for hunting a mammoth." //

NAME _____

CHECK YOUR UNDERSTANDING

A. Reread "Robert the Robot" on **Student Edition** pages 164–173. Then read each sentence below. Circle the letter of the correct answer.

1. The father wanted a robot that _____.

   A did homework   **C** played ball

   B was a lot of fun   **D** did chores

2. Robert the robot _____.

   A is smaller than a child   **C** is a machine

   B is a living thing   **D** looks like a person

ELPS 4.E read linguistically accommodated content area material • 4.G.3 demonstrate comprehension by responding to questions

79

NAME _____

B. Read each sentence below. Circle the letter of the correct answer.

3. The boy didn't like the robot at first because _____.

   A he wanted a different kind of robot

   B he didn't want a robot in the house at all

   C he wanted to buy computer games instead of a robot

   D the robot didn't follow Dad's commands

4. The first way the robot helped the boy was by _____.

   A doing one of his chores

   B driving him to school

   C making a really good dinner

   D making him scream

C. Read each question below. Circle the letter of the correct answer.

5. What caused the boy's feelings about the robot to change?

   A The robot showed that he could talk.

   B The robot liked to play games.

   C The robot turned out to be very helpful.

   D The robot did the boy's homework for him.

6. What is the one thing that Robert didn't understand?

   A He didn't understand how the stove worked.

   B He didn't understand the meaning of "lighten up."

   C He couldn't figure out how the car worked.

   D He couldn't figure out the answers to the boy's homework.

A. Label

Write a word that names each picture. Use a word from the word box.

bank	back	king	kick	him	hand	hats	jets

1. _____
2. _____
3. _____
4. _____

B. Phonics

Read these words aloud. Use the phonics skills you have learned.

	A	B	C	D	E	F	G
5.	skin	last	bank	toe	flip	baby	rapid
6.	stitch	mask	bang	tie	brain	logo	habit
7.	spoke	toast	sunk	foe	clap	total	timid
8.	snack	list	thing	dye	band	icon	valid
9.	smell	risk	rung	Joe	melt	veto	limit
10.	slide	gasp	think	woe	tree	minus	denim

C. High-Frequency Words

Read these words aloud.

11.	when	your	can	said	there	use
12.	an	each	which	she	do	how

ELPS 2.B recognize elements of the English sound system in newly acquired vocabulary • 3.A practice producing sounds of newly acquired vocabulary • 4.A.1 learn relationships between sounds and letters of the English language • 4.C.1 develop basic sight vocabulary • 5.A learn relationships between sounds and letters when writing in English • 5.C.1 spell familiar English words • 5.C.2 employ English spelling patterns • 5.C.3 employ English spelling rules

NAME _____

D. Listen. Read. Check.

Your teacher will say a word. Mark the box next to the word.

13.	☐ laid	☐ lad	☐ lady
14.	☐ cave	☐ cabinet	☐ cabin
15.	☐ sell	☐ smell	☐ melts
16.	☐ ask	☐ ax	☐ sax
17.	☐ rink	☐ ring	☐ Rick
18.	☐ sank	☐ sang	☐ sand
19.	☐ time	☐ tide	☐ tie
20.	☐ toad	☐ toe	☐ to

E. Spelling

Your teacher will say a word. Write the word. Check your spelling.

21. _____   23. _____

22. _____   24. _____

ELPS 2.B recognize elements of the English sound system in newly acquired vocabulary • 3.A practice producing sounds of newly acquired vocabulary • 4.A.1 learn relationships between sounds and letters of the English language • 4.C.1 develop basic sight vocabulary • 5.A learn relationships between sounds and letters when writing in English • 5.C.1 spell familiar English words • 5.C.2 employ English spelling patterns • 5.C.3 employ English spelling rules

NAME ——————————————————————————

CHECKLIST

Word	I've never heard of it.	I've heard of it.	I know what it means.
solar system	☐	☐	☐
planet	☐	☐	☐
orbit	☐	☐	☐
phase	☐	☐	☐
outer space	☐	☐	☐
astronaut	☐	☐	☐

Which word did you find most challenging?

——————————————————————————————

ELPS 1.C use strategic learning techniques to acquire basic and grade-level vocabulary

NAME _____

CHECKLIST

Word	I've never heard of it.	I've heard of it.	I know what it means.
gravity	☐	☐	☐
train	☐	☐	☐
weightless	☐	☐	☐
crew	☐	☐	☐
experience	☐	☐	☐
space shuttle	☐	☐	☐

Which word did you find most interesting?

_____

NAME —————————————————————————

READING LONGER WORDS

> ### Reading Syllables with a VCe Letter Pattern
>
> Read these words: *hope, bike, Pete, same, cube.* They all have a vowel + a consonant + silent e. Look for this letter pattern in longer words.

> ### You can divide:
> - between the words in a compound word.
> - after a prefix, or before a suffix.
> - between the consonants in a VCCV letter pattern.
> - before or after the consonant in a VCV letter pattern.

A. Divide the word. Circle the VCe letter pattern. Read each syllable. Then read the whole word.

erase	unite	locate
donate	refine	refuse

B. Divide the word. Circle the VCe letter pattern. Read each syllable. Then read the whole word.

inflate	dislike	mistake	exhale

C. Divide the word. Circle the VCe letter pattern. Read each syllable. Then read the whole word.

divide	decade	volume

D. Divide the word. Circle the VCe letter pattern. Read each syllable. Then read the whole word.

reptile	confuse	invite	escape
update	bedtime	online	inside

© HMH Supplemental Publishers Inc.

ELPS 4.A.1 learn relationships between sounds and letters of the English language • 4.A.2 decode words using a combination of skills

NAME _____

REPORT RUBRIC

When you write a report, check it against this rubric. Did you do all you can to make it good?

Report
The report is about one topic, or subject.
The report includes important details about the topic.
If the report includes a problem, it explains the solution to the problem.
There is a conclusion that summarizes the report's main idea.
The report is written neatly to make it easy to read.
There are different kinds of sentences, and the sentences do not all start with the same word.
The report uses correct grammar, spelling, and punctuation.

© HMH Supplemental Publishers Inc.

ELPS 1.B.2 monitor written language production and employ self-corrective techniques • 4.D use prereading supports to enhance comprehension of written text • 5.D.1 edit writing for standard grammar and usage, including subject-verb agreement • 5.D.2 edit writing for standard grammar and usage, including pronoun agreement • 5.D.3 edit writing for standard grammar and usage, including appropriate verb tenses • 5.F.1 write using a variety of grade-appropriate sentence lengths • 5.F.2 write using a variety of grade-appropriate sentence patterns • 5.F.3 write using a variety of grade-appropriate connecting words • 5.G.2 describe with increasing specificity and detail to fulfill content area writing needs • 5.G.3 explain with increasing specificity and detail to fulfill content area writing needs

NAME —————————————————————

PROBLEM AND SOLUTION ORGANIZER

 A report gives facts about a topic. Some facts may describe a problem. Other facts give the solution. Finally, a report has a conclusion, or ending. This conclusion tells the main idea in a new way.

Topic ————————————————————————

Problem	Solution

Conclusion ————————————————————

———————————————————————————

———————————————————————————

© HMH Supplemental Publishers Inc.

ELPS 4.D use prereading supports to enhance comprehension of written text • 5.G.2 describe with increasing specificity and detail to fulfill content area writing needs • 5.G.3 explain with increasing specificity and detail to fulfill content area writing needs

87

NAME _____

CAPITALIZE THE FIRST WORD OF A SENTENCE

 Every sentence begins with a capital letter.

Make sure you capitalize the first word of a sentence.
People have visited outer space.
There are billions of stars.

Write each sentence correctly.

1. today, our class studied space travel.

_____

2. *apollo 11* landed on the Moon.

_____

3. the ship landed on July 20, 1969.

_____

4. three astronauts were the crew.

_____

5. one of the astronauts was Neil Armstrong.

_____

6. the others were Buzz Aldrin and Michael Collins.

_____

NAME

EDITING FOR GRAMMAR, SPELLING, AND PUNCTUATION

See also pages 180 and 181.

A verb must agree with its subject.
I am here.   *She is here.*   *We are here.*

The present progressive form of a verb shows a continuing action. It uses *am, is,* or *are* and a verb that ends in –*ing.*
I am eating lunch.   *They are going away.*

The future tense of a verb shows action that will happen in the future. It uses the helping verb *will* plus the main verb.
Tomorrow we will visit my aunt.

Listen to your teacher. Compare the first draft of a report to the edited draft.

First Draft

Long ago, people saw shapes in groups of stars. (these) shapes are called constellations. One constellation is called Orion. It (look) like a warrior. It has a club and a shield. It has a belt made of three stars. A sword hangs from the belt. Today, as people (is) looking at the night sky, they see the same constellations. (people) in the future will (looked) at the same constellations. The stars will shine for a very long time.

Edited Draft

Long ago, people saw shapes in groups of stars. These shapes are called constellations. One constellation is called Orion. It looks like a warrior. It has a club and a shield. It has a belt made of three stars. A sword hangs from the belt. Today, as people are looking at the night sky, they see the same constellations. People in the future will look at the same constellations. The stars will shine for a very long time.

© HMH Supplemental Publishers Inc.

ELPS 5.D.1 edit writing for standard grammar and usage, including subject-verb agreement • 5.D.3 edit writing for standard grammar and usage, including appropriate verb tenses • 5.E employ increasingly complex grammatical structures in content area writing

89

NAME _____

READER'S LOG: "THE SUN AND THE STARS"

> (i) Active listeners take notes. Active readers do, too. Write only what you need to remember the important information.

PAIR AND SHARE Reread the selection with your partner. Mark the boxes and take notes as you read. Add to your notes as you talk to your partner.

1. How difficult is the selection?

   ☐ very difficult   ☐ not too difficult   ☐ easy

2. What makes the selection difficult?

   ☐ the words   ☐ the information   ☐ everything!

3. List the difficult words.

_____

4. What did you do about those words?

   ☐ We talked about them.   ☐ We looked them up in a dictionary.

   ☐ We looked at the pictures.   ☐ We asked our teacher.

5. What did you and your partner already know?

Me	My partner	
☐	☐	a lot about the sun and the stars
☐	☐	something about the sun and the stars
☐	☐	very little—the information was new

6. How did you use the photos? Did they help you?

7. Are there any sentences that you don't understand?
   Note the page number, and ask your teacher what they mean. _____

ELPS 2.I.5 demonstrate listening comprehension by taking notes • 4.E read linguistically accommodated content area material • 4.F.6 use support from peers and teachers to read content area text • 4.F.7 use support from peers and teachers to confirm understanding • 4.F.8 use support from peers and teachers to develop vocabulary • 4.F.9 use support from peers and teachers to develop language structures • 4.F.10 use support from peers and teachers to develop background knowledge • 4.G.1 demonstrate comprehension by participating in shared reading • 4.G.4 demonstrate comprehension of English by taking notes

NAME ————————————————————————

WHICH WORD?

Write the vocabulary word from the box to complete each sentence.

planet	phase	solar system	astronaut
	orbit	outer space	

1. The planets _____ the Sun.

_____

2. The Sun, the Moon, and the planets are in the _____.

_____

3. A person who travels in space is an _____.

_____

4. The planets and the stars are in _____.

_____

5. Each _____ of the Moon is a different shape.

_____

6. A _____ is a large object that moves around the Sun.

_____

NAME _____

MATCH IT UP

Write the letter of the definition that matches each word.

1. _____ weightless   **A** a team of people working together

2. _____ experience   **B** the force that pulls an object to Earth

3. _____ crew   **C** to practice to get better at something

4. _____ space shuttle   **D** a spacecraft that makes more than one trip

5. _____ gravity   **E** without having gravity pulling it down

6. _____ train   **F** to take part in an event

NAME _____

A. Asking Questions

Look at the picture. Which question best fits the picture?

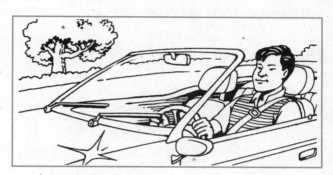

1. What is the best question?

   A Who are you?

   B What is the girl saying?

   C How much is it?

1. What is the best question?

   A Where is he going?

   B What is Mom doing?

   C Do you like cars?

B. Choosing the Verb Tense

Read the sentence. Which verb tense is used?

3. The girl is kicking the ball.

   A present tense

   B future tense

   C past tense

4. Yesterday, my brother helped me.

   A present tense

   B future tense

   C past tense

ELPS 4.C.3 comprehend English vocabulary in written classroom materials • 4.C.4 comprehend English language structures in written classroom materials • 4.F.4 use visual and contextual support

93

NAME _____

C. Present or Present Progressive Tense

Look at the picture. Read the sentences. Circle the letter of the BEST sentence to describe the picture.

5. A They are talking about their plans.

B They sometimes write stories.

6. Tell why you think the sentence you chose is best.

_____

_____

_____

_____

_____

PAIR AND SHARE Discuss what you do every day and what you are doing right now. Use these sentence frames:

A. Ask questions.

1. *What do you do every day?*
2. *What are you doing right now?*

B. Answer the questions.

1. *Every day, I _____.* (eat breakfast, read books, study math, talk to friends)

2. *Right now, I am _____.* (talking to you, doing my homework, sitting in class)

Check page 180 to review the simple present tense and the present progressive action verbs.

Monitor Language: How's your grammar?

Listen to your partner. Were the present and present progressive verb forms correct?

Yes, always	Sometimes	Never
☐	☐	☐

How were your verb tenses and forms? Were they correct?

Yes, always	Sometimes	Never
☐	☐	☐

ELPS 3.C.1 speak using a variety of grammatical structures • 3.C.2 speak using a variety of sentence lengths • 3.C.3 speak using a variety of sentence types • 4.C.3 comprehend English vocabulary in written classroom materials • 4.C.4 comprehend English language structures in written classroom materials • 4.F.4 use visual and contextual support • 4.F.9 use support from peers and teachers to develop language structures

NAME _____

ACTIVE READING OF THE TEXT

 Self-monitor your understanding as you read.

1. **Reread.** Start with the last sentence you understood. Then read on from that point.

2. **Take notes.** Write down the most important details. This can help you understand and remember what you read.

3. **Look up words you don't know.**

4. **Ask questions.** Then look for answers to your questions in the text, or you can ask someone.

From "Traveling Through Space"	Active Reading
The closest object in outer space is the Moon. It's not easy to get there! In fact, only twelve people have ever been on the Moon. And nobody has been there since 1972. The rocket *Apollo 11* carried the first crew of astronauts to the Moon. As the first man stepped onto the Moon's surface, he said, "One small step for man. One giant leap for mankind."	Underline anything you do not understand. Take notes. What are the most important ideas? _____ _____ _____ Tell what you reread or a question you asked. _____ _____ _____

ELPS 4.E read linguistically accommodated content area material • 4.G.4 demonstrate comprehension English by taking notes

95

NAME _____

READ FOR RATE

Read aloud the following passage from "Patterns in the Stars." Have a partner time your reading for one minute. Then, fill in the chart at the bottom of the page with the number of words you read. Read the passage a second and third time. Try to increase the number of words you read accurately in a minute.

The stars all look very much alike. Each one is a point of	13
light in the night sky. We can tell which star is which by the	27
patterns that the stars make in the sky.	35
The patterns of stars are called constellations. Long ago,	44
people gave them names. These were names of animals or of	55
people. Often, the characters were parts of stories.	63
The Great Bear is lowest in the sky in the fall. American	75
Indians said that it was because the bear was looking for a	87
place to sleep for the winter.	93

Number of Words Read		
First Reading	Second Reading	Third Reading

NAME _____

CHECK YOUR UNDERSTANDING

A. Read the following questions about "Traveling Through Space" on Student Edition pages 220–225. Then read each sencence. Circle the letter of the correct answer.

1. Astronauts in space _____.

    A float   **C** can run faster

    B glow   **D** become very heavy

2. The Voyager space probes fly _____.

    A on the Moon   **C** to Mars

    B under the water   **D** more than 10 billion miles from Earth

ELPS 4.E read linguistically accommodated content area material • 4.G.3 demonstrate comprehension by responding to questions

97

NAME _____

B. Reread "The Sun and the Stars" on **Student Edition** pages 210–219. Then read each sentence below. Circle the letter of the correct answer.

3. Planets orbit the sun because of the sun's _____.

  A light   **C** heat

  B huge flames   **D** gravity

4. A light year is a way to measure _____.

  A heat   **C** brightness

  B distance   **D** a planet's mass

C. Read each question about "The Sun and the Stars." Circle the letter of the correct answer.

5. What do we know now about the universe?

  A We can't measure its size.

  B It has an edge.

  C It is part of the Milky Way.

  D It is shaped like a spiral.

6. What can we infer about our sun?

  A It is one of the brightest stars in our galaxy.

  B It is many light years away from Earth.

  C It will always stay the size it is now.

  D It is smaller than some other stars.

ELPS 4.E read linguistically accommodated content area material • 4.G.3 demonstrate comprehension by responding to questions

NAME _____

A. Label

Write a word that names each picture. Use a word from the word box.

bread	bed	con	hockey	hook
coin	box	toll		

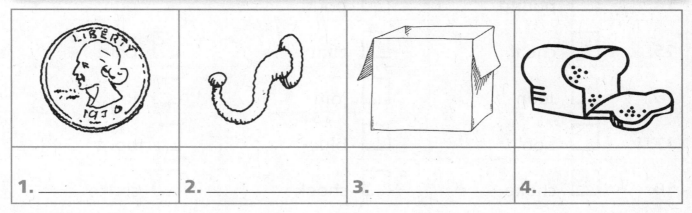

1. _____ 2. _____ 3. _____ 4. _____

B. Phonics

Read these words aloud. Use the phonics skills you have learned.

	A	B	C	D	E	F	G
5.	toy	stew	found	tea	book	moon	notebook
6.	soy	blue	house	sea	cook	troop	excite
7.	boy	chew	mouse	pea	rook	room	female
8.	coin	glue	loud	seat	took	cool	tadpole
9.	soil	few	out	bead	hook	proof	escape
10.	coil	true	about	treat	look	hoop	unmade

C. High-Frequency Words

Read these words aloud.

11.	their	if	will	up	other	about
12.	out	many	them	all	these	some

ELPS 2.B recognize elements of the English sound system in newly acquired vocabulary • 3.A practice producing sounds of newly acquired vocabulary • 4.A.1 learn relationships between sounds and letters of the English language • 4.C.1 develop basic sight vocabulary • 5.A learn relationships between sounds and letters when writing in English • 5.C.1 spell familiar English words • 5.C.2 employ English spelling pattern • 5.C.3 employ English spelling rules

NAME _____

D. Listen. Read. Check.

Your teacher will say a word. Mark the box next to the word.

13.	☐ few	☐ food	☐ foot
14.	☐ pound	☐ pond	☐ pun
15.	☐ cheat	☐ chat	☐ Chet
16.	☐ Joan	☐ join	☐ joy
17.	☐ boo	☐ blue	☐ boot
18.	☐ choke	☐ shook	☐ shake
19.	☐ sun	☐ soon	☐ sound
20.	☐ joke	☐ go	☐ Joe

E. Spelling

Your teacher will say a word. Write the word. Check your spelling.

21. _____   23. _____

22. _____   24. _____

ELPS 2.B recognize elements of the English sound system in newly acquired vocabulary • 3.A practice producing sounds of newly acquired vocabulary • 4.A.1 learn relationships between sounds and letters of the English language • 4.C.1 develop basic sight vocabulary • 5.A learn relationships between sounds and letters when writing in English • 5.C.1 spell familiar English words • 5.C.2 employ English spelling pattern • 5.C.3 employ English spelling rules

NAME ———————————————————————————————————

CHECKLIST

Word	I've never heard of it.	I've heard of it.	I know what it means.
natural resources	☐	☐	☐
energy	☐	☐	☐
oil	☐	☐	☐
pollute	☐	☐	☐
conserve	☐	☐	☐
careless	☐	☐	☐

Which word did you find most challenging?

———————————————————————————————————

NAME _____

CHECKLIST

Word	I've never heard of it.	I've heard of it.	I know what it means.
creek	☐	☐	☐
gallon	☐	☐	☐
recycle	☐	☐	☐
garbage	☐	☐	☐
chemical	☐	☐	☐
harm	☐	☐	☐

Which word did you find most interesting?

_____

ELPS 1.C. use strategic learning techniques to acquire basic and grade-level vocabulary

NAME ——————————————————————————

READING LONGER WORDS

Reading Vowel Pair Syllables

Two vowel letters often stand for one sound.

Examples: *keep, bead, goat, paid, sound*

You can divide:

- between the words in a compound word.
- after a prefix, or before a suffix.
- between the consonants in a VCCV letter pattern.
- before or after the consonant in a VCV letter pattern.

A. Divide the word. Circle the vowel pair. Read each syllable. Then read the whole word.

n e e d e d	l o u d l y	w e e k l y
w o o d e n	b r a i d e d	s l e e p i n g

B. Divide the word. Circle the vowel pair. Read each syllable. Then read the whole word.

n o t e b o o k	p e a n u t	c l a s s r o o m	h a n d r a i l
r o w b o a t	t e x t b o o k	c u t o u t	b o w t i e

C. Divide the word. Read each syllable. Then read the whole word.

b e l o w	m e a d o w	e m u

D. Divide the word. Read each syllable. Then read the whole word.

e l b o w	m u s h r o o m	s h a m p o o	e x p l a i n
r o w b o a t	w i n d o w	r a i n b o w	i g l o o

ELPS 4.A.1 learn relationships between sounds and letters • 4.A.2 decode words using a combination of skills

NAME _____

COMPARISON RUBRIC

When you write a comparison, check it against this rubric. Did you do all you can to make it good?

Comparison
There is a topic sentence. This sentence tells what the writer is comparing.
The writer gives details that tell how the topics are alike.
The writer gives details that tell how the topics are different.
There is a sentence at the end that summarizes what the writing is about.
The writing is neat and easy to read.
The writer uses correct grammar, spelling, and punctuation.

ELPS 1.B.2 monitor written language production and employ self-corrective techniques • 4.D use prereading supports to enhance comprehension of written text • 5.D.1 edit writing for standard grammar and usage, including subject-verb agreement • 5.D.2 edit writing for standard grammar and usage, including pronoun agreement • 5.D.3 edit writing for standard grammar and usage, including appropriate verb tenses • 5.G.2 describe with increasing specificity and detail to fulfill content area writing needs • 5.G.3 explain with increasing specificity and detail to fulfill content area writing needs

NAME _____

COMPARISON ORGANIZER

 When you compare and contrast, you tell how things are alike and how they are different.

 You can use a Venn diagram to compare and contrast. Each oval stands for one item.

Write facts that are only true for one item in its oval.

Write facts that are only true about the other item in its oval.

Write facts that are true for both items in the space where the ovals overlap.

Complete the diagram. Then summarize your ideas about the two items.

Item _____   Item _____

Summary

_____

_____

ELPS 4.D use prereading supports to enhance comprehension of written text • 5.G.2 describe with increasing specificity and detail to fulfill content area writing needs

105

NAME _____

USING COMMAS IN SENTENCES

> **Commas tell a reader where to pause. There are several rules for using commas.**
>
> Use commas to separate three or more items in a series. *Computers, cell phones, and calculators make life easier.*
>
> Use a comma to separate the parts of a compound sentence *Cell phones make keeping in touch easier, and calculators make math easier.*
>
> Use a comma after the words yes and no when they begin a sentence. *Yes, I love computers!*
>
> Use a comma to set off the name of a person you are speaking to. *Marie, please print a copy of your report.*

Write each sentence correctly. Use commas where needed.

1. Cars can carry one two or more people.

_____

2. Rita does your bike have gears?

_____

3. I will drive and Judy will ride her bike.

_____

4. I will research boats and bikes.

_____

5. No we can't stop now.

_____

NAME —————————————————————————————————

EDITING FOR GRAMMAR, SPELLING, AND PUNCTUATION

See also pages 175 and 177.

> ⓘ The verb *make* is regular in the present tense. The verbs *go*, *do*, and *have* are irregular in the present tense.

I	make	go	do	have
You	make	go	do	have
He, she, it	makes	**goes**	**does**	**has**

> ⓘ The verbs *go*, *do*, *have*, and *make* are irregular in the past tense.

Verb	go	do	have	make
Past Tense	went	did	had	made

> ⓘ Form the possessive of most singular nouns by adding *'s*.
> the dog's bone   my sister's car

Listen to your teacher. Compare the first draft of a comparison to the final draft.

Today, I made a peanut butter sandwich for lunch. My sister (maked) a turkey sandwich. We both started with bread, but the other parts were different. I (haved) grape jelly with peanut butter ᴧand my (sisters) sandwich had cheese and lettuce. Both were tasty ᴧand they both (goed) (quick)!

———————————————————————————————————

Today, I made a peanut butter sandwich for lunch. My sister made a turkey sandwich. We both started with bread, but the other parts were different. I had grape jelly with peanut butter, and my sister's sandwich had cheese and lettuce. Both were tasty, and they both went quickly!

ELPS 5.D.1 edit writing for standard grammar and usage, including subject-verb agreement • 5.E employ increasingly complex grammatical structures in content area writing

NAME _____

READER'S LOG: "MISTER TWISTER"

BEFORE READING: PAIR AND SHARE

1. My class talked about the _____.
   ☐ title   ☐ illustrations   ☐ background information

2. I understood _____ of the background information.
   ☐ most or all   ☐ some   ☐ little or none

DURING READING

3. What opinion of Mister Twister does the writer have? Explain.

   _____

   _____

   _____

4. Is there anything in the story that you do not understand? Write about it here:

   _____

   _____

AFTER READING: PAIR AND SHARE

5. Talk to your partner about anything that you did not understand.

Now, my partner and I understand _____.

Me   ☐ a lot better ☐ a little better ☐ no better

My partner   ☐ a lot better ☐ a little better ☐ no better

ELPS 4.E read linguistically accommodated content area material • 4.F.6 use support from peers and teachers to read content area text • 4.F.7 use support from peers and teachers to confirm understanding • 4.F.10 use support from peers and teachers to develop background knowledge

NAME —————————————————————————————

USE CLUES

Read each sentence. Use context clues to help you figure out the correct vocabulary word from the box that completes each sentence. Write the word on the line.

| energy | oil | natural resources | conserve | careless | pollute |

1. My brother was very ——— and knocked a glass of water off the table.

———————————————————————————————————

2. The gas that cars use is made from ———.

———————————————————————————————————

3. The more people ———, the less healthy the Earth is.

———————————————————————————————————

4. Oil, air, water, and wood are ——— on Earth.

———————————————————————————————————

5. It takes ——— to run most of the machines in a house.

———————————————————————————————————

6. I turn off the lights so that I ——— electricity.

———————————————————————————————————

NAME _____

WHICH WORD AM I?

Read the clues. Write the correct vocabulary word from the box to match each clue.

chemical	recycle	gallon	garbage	creek	harm

1. I am the act of making sure that things can be used again.

_____

2. I am a material made by people.

_____

3. I am the act of hurting something.

_____

4. I am something that people do not want or need anymore.

_____

5. I am a small stream of water.

_____

6. I am used to measure liquids.

_____

ELPS 4.C.3 comprehend English vocabulary in written classroom materials

NAME ——

A. Subject and Object Pronouns

Look at the picture. Read the sentence. Which word can replace the underlined words?

1. Anna kicks <u>the ball</u>!

   A she   **C** it

   B her   **D** them

2. <u>My parents</u> make the dinner.

   A Them   **C** It

   B They   **D** He

B. Combining Sentences

Which sentence **best** combines the information in the first two sentences?

3. Mr. Kim has a lot of books. I like his books.

   A I like Mr. Kim's books.

   B They are Mr. Kims books.

   C I like books.

4. The baby has toys. They are broken.

   A The babys toys are broken.

   B The baby's toys are broken.

   C Break the baby's toys.

ELPS 4.C.3 comprehend English vocabulary in written classroom materials • 4.C.4 comprehend English language structures in written classroom materials • 4.F.4 use visual and contextual support

111

NAME _____

C. Irregular Past-Tense Verbs

Choose the verb that best fits the sentence.

7. They sing very loud.
   Last week, they _____ in a concert.

   A sing   C is singing

   B sang   D will sing

8. My brother makes popcorn.
   Last week, he _____ a big mess!

   A make   C will make

   B makes   D made

PAIR AND SHARE With your partner, discuss what each of you or one other person owns.

Use these sentence frames:

A. Ask a question.

   Whose _____ is that? (book, pencil, pen, car)

B. Answer the question.

   That is _____. (Miguel's book, the teacher's desk, my mother's jacket)

Check page 177 to review how to say that someone owns something. Be sure to pronounce the *'s*.

Monitor Language: How's your grammar?

Listen to your partner. Was the correct possessive form used? Was the *'s* pronounced?

Yes, always	Sometimes	Never
☐	☐	☐

How were your possessive forms? Were they correct? Did you pronounce *'s*?

Yes, always	Sometimes	Never
☐	☐	☐

ELPS 3.C.1 speak using a variety of grammatical structures • 3.C.2 speak using a variety of sentence lengths • 3.C.3 speak using a variety of sentence types • 4.C.3 comprehend English vocabulary in written classroom materials • 4.C.4 comprehend English language structures in written classroom materials • 4.F.4 use visual and contextual support • 4.F.9 use support from peers and teachers to develop language structures

NAME _____

ACTIVE READING OF THE TEXT

 Self-monitor your understanding as you read.

1. **Reread**. Start with the last sentence you understood. Then read on from that point.

2. **Take notes**. Write down the most important details. This can help you understand and remember what you read.

3. **Look up words you don't know.**

4. **Ask questions**. Then look for answers to your questions in the text, or you can ask someone.

From "Don't Waste"	Active Reading
A lot of things in your home use energy. The lights and the television use electricity. The heat and hot water use electricity or oil. We need to conserve oil. What about electricity? Most of the electricity in this country is made using coal. We need to conserve coal, too. So, don't waste electricity. Another resource you use at home is water. The water probably comes from a long way away. Making water clean uses energy. So, don't waste water. There's another reason not to waste. You save money!	Underline anything you do not understand. Take notes. What are the most important ideas? _____ _____ Tell what you reread or a question you asked. _____ _____

© HMH Supplemental Publishers Inc.

ELPS 4.E read linguistically accommodated content area material • 4.G.4 demonstrate comprehension of English by taking notes

113

NAME _____

READ WITH EXPRESSION

Read the poem "Help!" aloud. Read with energy and strong emotion. Pause for punctuation marks such as commas and periods. Listen to your partner's reading. Then practice the passage a second time.

Note: One slash (/) indicates a short pause for a comma or a dash. Two slashes (//) indicates that you stop for a period, question mark, or exclamation point.

Look at that chimney— / all that smoke, /
The air around is airless! //
It's so bad all the trees will choke. //
How can we be so careless? //

Look at the mess dumped in the creek. //
There's no point going fishing. //
It's getting worse here, / week by week. //
It won't be cured by wishing. //

Look at the trash by the side of the road, /
At the dead crops on the farm. //
It hasn't rained or even snowed. //
Someone pull the earth alarm! //

NAME _____

CHECK YOUR UNDERSTANDING

A. Reread "Mister Twister" on **Student Edition** pages 256–265. Then read each sentence below. Circle the letter of the correct answer.

1. Mr. Twister harms the forest by _____.

   A starting a fire   **C** cutting down trees

   B building too many factories   **D** using too much oil

2. Mr. Twister's big car wastes _____.

   A wood   **C** trees

   B cans   **D** gas

ELPS 4.E read linguistically accommodated content area material • 4.G.3 demonstrate comprehension by responding to questions

115

NAME _____

B. Read each sentence below. Circle the letter of the correct answer.

3. Mr. Twister can waste less at home by _____.

   A sorting and recycling trash   **C** making less money

   B doing without tires   **D** using cans instead of bottles

4. Mr. Twister's tires are harmful because _____.

   A he puts too many on his car   **C** he burns them

   B he throws them away in too   **D** he dumps chemicals on them
       many places

C. Read the following questions about "Don't Waste" on **Student Edition** pages 266–271. Then read each question below. Circle the letter of the correct answer.

5. What question does this selection answer?

   A How does a washing machine work?

   B What other ways can you keep clothes clean?

   C Where is the greatest amount of electricity used in a home?

   D What things can all of us conserve at home?

6. How does using water use up energy?

   A Saving water costs you less.

   B It takes energy to clean water after it's used.

   C Keeping the refrigerator door open uses up electricity.

   D Cold water uses up more energy than hot water.

ELPS 4.E read linguistically accommodated content area material • 4.G.3 demonstrate comprehension by responding to questions

NAME —————————————————————————

A. Label

Write a word that names the picture. Use a word from the word box.

crow	cow	car	star	hook	foot	fur	core

1. _____
2. _____
3. _____
4. _____

B. Phonics

Read the words aloud. Use the phonics skills you have learned.

	A	B	C	D	E	F	G
5.	crow	cow	car	soar	bird	burn	railroad
6.	show	now	tar	more	fern	fir	dugout
7.	blow	wow	start	porch	word	herd	proceed
8.	grow	town	part	score	fur	stir	release
9.	low	owl	chart	for	sir	purr	repeat
10.	slow	how	lark	poor	turn	her	midweek

C. High-Frequency Words

Read these words aloud.

11.	her	would	make	like	him	into
12.	time	has	look	two	more	write

ELPS 2.B recognize elements of the English sound system in newly acquired vocabulary • 3.A practice producing sounds of newly acquired vocabulary • 4.A.1 learn relationships between sounds and letters of the English language • 4.C.1 develop basic sight vocabulary • 5.A learn relationships between sounds and letters when writing in English • 5.C.1 spell familiar English words • 5.C.2 employ English spelling pattern • 5.C.3 employ English spelling rules

NAME _____

D. Listen. Read. Check.

Your teacher will say a word. Mark the box next to the word.

13.	☐ mark		☐ make		☐ mock
14.	☐ dirt		☐ date		☐ dart
15.	☐ crow		☐ row		☐ cow
16.	☐ sow		☐ slow		☐ low
17.	☐ sir		☐ sore		☐ shark
18.	☐ herd		☐ her		☐ hurt
19.	☐ park		☐ part		☐ par
20.	☐ sheer		☐ sharp		☐ chart

E. Spelling

Your teacher will say a word. Write the word. Check your spelling.

21. _____   23. _____

22. _____   24. _____

ELPS 2.B recognize elements of the English sound system in newly acquired vocabulary • 3.A practice producing sounds of newly acquired vocabulary • 4.A.1 learn relationships between sounds and letters of the English language • 4.C.1 develop basic sight vocabulary • 5.A learn relationships between sounds and letters when writing in English • 5.C.1 spell familiar English words • 5.C.2 employ English spelling pattern • 5.C.3 employ English spelling rules

NAME —————————————————————————————

MONITORING LISTENING CHECKLIST

	Unit 7	Unit 8	End of Book
	We the People	In the Money	
1. What is the topic?			
2. The general meaning of the discussion was ____.			
3. The words and sentences were mostly ____.	☐ clear ☐ confusing	☐ clear ☐ confusing	☐ clear ☐ confusing
4. Some of the important details include ____.			
5. I ____ ask for help when I don't understand.	☐ usually ☐ sometimes ☐ never	☐ usually ☐ sometimes ☐ never	☐ usually ☐ sometimes ☐ never
6. The way I understand discussions has ____.	☐ improved ☐ stayed the same	☐ improved ☐ stayed the same	☐ improved ☐ stayed the same

ELPS 2.D.1 monitor understanding of spoken language • 2.D.2 seek clarification [of spoken language] as needed • 2.G.7 understand important details; focus on topics • 2.G.8 understand important details; focus on language • 2.G.9 understand important details; focus on contexts • 2.H.1 understand implicit ideas • 2.H.2 understand Information

119

NAME _____

CHECKLIST

Word	I've never heard of it.	I've heard of it.	I know what it means.
citizen	☐	☐	☐
vote	☐	☐	☐
election	☐	☐	☐
campaign	☐	☐	☐
community	☐	☐	☐
responsible	☐	☐	☐

Which word did you find most challenging?

_____

NAME ——————————————————————————

CHECKLIST

Word	I've never heard of it.	I've heard of it.	I know what it means.
problem	☐	☐	☐
solution	☐	☐	☐
advice	☐	☐	☐
present	☐	☐	☐
speech	☐	☐	☐
city council	☐	☐	☐

Which word did you find most interesting?

——

NAME _____

MONITORING SPEAKING CHECKLIST

	Unit 7	Unit 8	End of Book
	The Coat	**Art Test**	
1. I can retell the story by describing the ____.	☐ beginning ☐ middle ☐ end	☐ beginning ☐ middle ☐ end	☐ beginning ☐ middle ☐ end
2. I can support my opinions, ideas, and feelings about the story ____.	☐ all of the time ☐ often ☐ sometimes	☐ all of the time ☐ often ☐ sometimes	☐ all of the time ☐ often ☐ sometimes
3. I can describe and explain what I want to say ____.	☐ all of the time ☐ often ☐ sometimes	☐ all of the time ☐ often ☐ sometimes	☐ all of the time ☐ often ☐ sometimes
4. The way I can make myself understood has ____.	☐ improved ☐ stayed the same ☐ gotten worse	☐ improved ☐ stayed the same ☐ gotten worse	☐ improved ☐ stayed the same ☐ gotten worse
5. How do you explain your answer to #4, above?			

© HMH Supplemental Publishers Inc.

ELPS 2.I.2 demonstrate listening comprehension by retelling or summarizing • 3.B.1 identify and describe people, places, and objects • 3.B.2 retell stories supported by pictures • 3.G.1 express opinions • 3.G.2 express ideas • 3.G.3 express feelings • 3.H.1 narrate with increasing specificity and detail • 3.H.2 describe with increasing specificity and detail • 3.H.3 explain with increasing specificity and detail

NAME ——————————————————————————————

READING LONGER WORDS

 Reading Syllables with Vowel + *r*

When a vowel is followed by the letter *r*, the sound of the vowel sometimes changes.

Examples: *her, bird, girl, pearl, cart, cork*

 You can divide:

- between the words in a compound word
- after a prefix or before a suffix
- between the consonants in a VCCV letter pattern
- before or after the consonant in a VCV letter pattern

A. Divide the word. Read each syllable. Then read the whole word.

started	curling	artist	taller	worker

B. Divide the word. Read each syllable. Then read the whole word.

birthday	bluebird	homework
offshore	pitchfork	boxcar

C. Divide the word. Read each syllable. Then read the whole word.

diner	baker	tiger
liver	ever	cower

D. Divide the word. Read each syllable. Then read the whole word. Remember: Digraphs such as *ch*, *th*, and *sh* act as one letter.

concert	turnip	further	burger

© HMH Supplemental Publishers Inc.

ELPS 4.A.1 learn relationships between sounds and letters of the English language • 4.A.2 decode words using a combination of skills

123

NAME _____

PERSUASIVE ESSAY RUBRIC

When you write a persuasive essay, check it against this rubric. Did you do all you can to make it good?

Persuasive Essay
A title tells what the essay is about.
The writer states an opinion.
The writer gives facts to support the opinion.
The facts are important and convincing.
It is clear what the writer wants readers to do.
The essay is written neatly to make it easy to read.
There are different kinds of sentences, and the sentences do not all start with the same word.
The grammar, spelling, and punctuation in the essay are correct.

© HMH Supplemental Publishers Inc.

ELPS 1.B.2 monitor written language production and employ self-corrective techniques • 4.D use prereading supports to enhance comprehension of written text • 5.D.1 edit writing for standard grammar and usage, including subject-verb agreement • 5.D.2 edit writing for standard grammar and usage, including pronoun agreement • 5.D.3 edit writing for standard grammar and usage, including appropriate verb tenses • 5.F.1 write using a variety of grade-appropriate sentence lengths • 5.F.2 write using a variety of grade-appropriate sentence patterns • 5.F.3 write using a variety of grade-appropriate connecting words • 5.G.3 explain with increasing specificity and detail to fulfill content area writing needs

NAME —————————————————————————

FACTS AND OPINIONS IN A PERSUASIVE ESSAY

> The purpose of a persuasive essay is to convince a reader to do something. First, identify the topic of your essay. Then state your opinion about the topic. You should list at least three facts that support your opinion. Include examples. At the end, you should restate your opinion. Finally, tell your readers what you want them to do.

Topic ———————————————————————

Opinion ——————————————————————

————————————————————————————

	Supporting Fact	Example
1		
2		
3		

Opinion ——————————————————————

Request ——————————————————————

ELPS 4.D use prereading supports to enhance comprehension of written text • 5.G.3 explain with increasing specificity and detail to fulfill content area writing needs

125

NAME _____

USING QUOTATION MARKS FOR SPEECH

 Use quotation marks to show a speaker's exact words.

Quotation marks go before and after a speaker's words.
"I like movies," said Ned.

Punctuation for a speaker's words goes inside the quotation marks. *"That's the best movie I've ever seen!" Anna said.*

A comma separates a speaker's words from the rest of the sentence. *Ned said, "Meet me outside the theater."*

A comma takes the place of a period inside quotation marks if it isn't the end of the whole sentence.
"I'll be there," Anna replied.

Write each sentence correctly.

1. My friend said, Let's go to the park.

_____

2. What about all this litter? I asked.

_____

3. Let's take garbage bags my friend said.

_____

4. Should we ask for help? I asked.

_____

5. Yes, let's ask all our friends my friend said.

_____

NAME ——————————————————————————————

EDITING FOR GRAMMAR, SPELLING, AND PUNCTUATION

See also pages 177, 178, and 182.

To show possession of a singular noun, add 's to the word.
Bill's dog   *the dog's tail*

To show possession of a plural noun ending in –s or –es, add an apostrophe to the end of the word. *the dogs' collars*

To show possession of a plural noun that does not end in –s or –es, add 's to the word. *the men's coats*

In English, we use only one negative word in a sentence.

Incorrect: *She could not find nothing to read.*
Correct: *She could find nothing to read.*
Correct: *She could not find anything to read.*

Listen to your teacher. Compare the first draft of a persuasive essay to the edited draft.

Everyone should play a sport. Take a (doctors) advice. Exercise is good for (peoples) health. It helps build strong muscles. It also builds a strong heart and lungs. You might say, "I don't need to play (no) sport. I already exercise.∧ But sports can also help in another way. Playing a sport can help you make friends. You can be part of a team. And you won't (never) run out of fun! So, play a sport today!

Everyone should play a sport. Take a doctor's advice. Exercise is good for people's health. It helps build strong muscles. It also builds a strong heart and lungs. You might say, "I don't need to play a sport. I already exercise." But sports can also help in another way. Playing a sport can help you make friends. You can be part of a team. And you won't ever run out of fun! So, play a sport today!

NAME _____

READER'S LOG: "HELPING THE COMMUNITY"

> ℹ️ Active listeners take notes. Active readers do, too. Write only the most important information.

PAIR AND SHARE Reread the selection with your partner. Mark the boxes and take notes as you read. Add to your notes as you talk to your partner.

1. How difficult is the selection?
   ☐ very difficult ☐ not too difficult ☐ easy

2. What makes the selection difficult?
   ☐ the words ☐ the information ☐ everything!

3. List the most difficult words.

_____

4. What did you do about the difficult words?
   ☐ We talked about them. ☐ We looked at the pictures.
   ☐ We looked them up in a dictionary. ☐ We asked our teacher.

5. What did you and your partner already know?

   Me   My partner
   ☐   ☐   a lot about people helping the community
   ☐   ☐   something about people helping the community
   ☐   ☐   very little—the information was new

6. How did you use the pictures? Did they help you?

_____

7. Are there any sentences that you don't understand?

   Note the page number, and ask your teacher what they mean. _____

ELPS 2.I.5 demonstrate listening comprehension by taking notes • 4.E read linguistically accommodated content area material • 4.F.6 use support from peers and teachers to read content area text • 4.F.7 use support from peers and teachers to confirm understanding • 4.F.8 use support from peers and teachers to develop vocabulary • 4.F.9 use support from peers and teachers to develop language structures • 4.F.10 use support from peers and teachers to develop background knowledge • 4.G.1 demonstrate comprehension by participating in shared reading • 4.G.4 demonstrate comprehension English by taking notes

NAME

UNSCRAMBLE THE WORDS

Unscramble each word to spell one of the words in the box. Write the word on the line under the scrambled word.

COMMUNITY	ELECTION	RESPONSIBLE
CAMPAIGN	VOTE	CITIZEN

1. PIGAMANC (a plan that a person follows to try to win an election)

_____

2. SEBLIPNOSER (doing the right thing)

_____

3. ETVO (to make a choice)

_____

4. IMMYNUTOC (a group of people who live in the same area)

_____

5. NETZICI (a person who lives in a certain city or country)

_____

6. OCLEENIT (a method of choosing a leader by voting)

_____

© HMH Supplemental Publishers Inc.

NAME _____

WHICH WORD?

Write the vocabulary word from the box to complete each sentence.

solution	speech	city council	problem	present	advice

1. A _____ causes trouble.

   _____

2. When you _____ a report, you read it to others.

   _____

3. Giving good _____ can help someone solve a problem.

   _____

4. The answer to a problem is a _____.

   _____

5. The _____ makes decisions about the city.

   _____

6. A politician may tell ideas to the people in a _____.

   _____

© HMH Supplemental Publishers Inc.

ELPS 4.C.3 comprehend English vocabulary in written classroom materials

NAME _____

A. Using Negatives

Look at the picture. Read the question. Circle the correct answer.

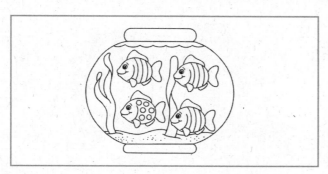

1. Are five goldfish in the bowl?

   A Yes, five goldfish are in the bowl.

   B No, five goldfish aren't in the bowl.

   C Yes, I see goldfish.

2. Is Lin in the house?

   A No, she isn't in the house.

   B Lin likes kites.

   C Nobody doesn't see nothing.

B. Plural Possessive Nouns

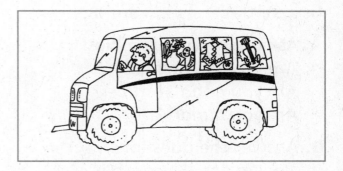

3. My two cousins own a cat. Is she cute?

   A No, my cat isn't cute.

   B Yes, my cousin's cat is cute.

   C Yes, my cousins' cat is cute.

4. Does this van belong to both of your parents?

   A No, it isn't my parents' van.

   B No, it isn't my parent's van.

   C Yes, I see my parents.

ELPS 4.C.1 develop basic sight vocabulary • 4.C.3 comprehend vocabulary used routinely in written classroom materials • 4.C.4 comprehend English language structures used in written classroom materials • 4.F.4 use visual and contextual support to develop grasp of language structures

131

NAME _____

C. Combining Sentences

Read the two sentences. Which sentence best combines the meaning of the two sentences?

5. The dog runs. The cats just sit.

  A John has a cat and dog.

  B The dog runs, but the cats just sit.

  C Dogs can't sit.

6. The book belongs to Sari. It belongs to her sister, too.

  A The book is theirs.

  B They are sitting there.

  C They can read.

PAIR AND SHARE Ask questions that can be answered *yes* or *no*. Use contractions in your answer.

A. Ask questions. Examples:
Are you 15 years old?
Are you good at soccer?
Are you hungry?

B. Answer the questions.
No, I'm not 15 years old.
Yes, I'm good at soccer.
No, I'm not hungry.

Check pages 171–172 to review using contractions.

Monitor Language: How's your grammar?

Listen to your partner. Was the question answered? Was a contraction used correctly?

Yes, always	Sometimes	Never
☐	☐	☐

Did you answer the question and correctly use contractions?

Yes, always	Sometimes	Never
☐	☐	☐

ELPS 3.C.1 speak using a variety of grammatical structures • 3.C.2 speak using a variety of sentence lengths • 3.C.3 speak using a variety of sentence types • 4.C.1 develop basic sight vocabulary • 4.C.3 comprehend English vocabulary in written classroom materials • 4.C.4 comprehend English language structures used in written classroom materials • 4.F.4 use visual and contextual support to develop grasp of language structures • 4.F.9 use support from peers and teachers to develop grasp of language structures

ACTIVE READING OF THE TEXT

Self-monitor your understanding as you read.

1. **Reread.** Start with the last sentences you understood. Then read on from that point.

2. **Take notes.** Write down the most important details. This can help you understand and remember what you read.

3. **Look up words you don't know.**

4. **Ask questions.** Then look for answers to your questions in the text, or you can ask someone.

From "Why Frank Picking Shouldn't Win"	Active Reading
I'm angry! I'll tell you why I'm angry. You know Frank Picking? Well, forget Frank Picking. He thinks he should be mayor. Well, he should not. He doesn't deserve to be mayor. Frank Picking's campaign is a joke. His speeches are all lies. He will say anything you want to hear. Do you want a new park for the city? He will promise you a new park. But he won't keep his promise.	Underline anything you do not understand. Take notes. What are the most important ideas? _____ _____ _____ Tell what you reread or a question you asked. _____ _____ _____

NAME _____

READ FOR ACCURACY

Work with a partner. Take turns reading the passage aloud. Try to speak clearly and pronounce each word correctly. Then review the passage together. Write the difficult words on the lines below. Practice saying the words aloud. Then read the passage a second time.

Lourdes was born in Cuba. Even so, she became a citizen of the United States. First, she had to live here for five years. She had to be able to read and write English.

When Lourdes was eighteen years old, she took an exam. She showed that she understood the way the United States works. Then Lourdes saw a judge who decided she could be a citizen.

Now Lourdes can vote in elections. And she does! She wants to have a say in how her city runs. She also votes in state elections and national elections.

_____   _____

_____   _____

_____   _____

_____   _____

_____   _____

NAME —————————————————————————————

CHECK YOUR UNDERSTANDING

A. Reread "Helping the Community" on **Student Edition** pages 302—311.
Then read each sentence below. Circle the letter of the correct answer.

1. You have to be an adult to _____.

   A pick up litter   **C** join 4-H

   B be a firefighter   **D** visit people in nursing homes

2. Kids can _____ to help people who don't have enough.

   A raise money   **C** recycle cans and bottles

   B keep the community safe   **D** work at an animal shelter

NAME _____

B. Read each sentence below. Circle the letter of the correct answer.

3. To recycle something means to get it ready to _____.

   A turn around and around   C be used again

   B be filled   D be thrown away

4. The largest group that the selection talks about is _____.

   A 4-H   C firefighters

   B scouts   D people who help in libraries

C. Read each question below. Circle the letter of the correct answer.

5. Which sentence from the story tells about jobs for adults?

   A There are clubs and groups you can join.

   B They study farming and science.

   C Groups sometimes help to clean up city parks.

   D Police officers help keep the community safe.

6. How are scouts and 4-H alike?

   A Members learn about farming.

   B Members learn first aid.

   C Members learn how to be leaders.

   D Both groups have the same number of members.

NAME _____

A. Label

Write a word that names the picture. Use a word from the word box.

chill	child	foal	fold	rid	car	fur	words

1. _____ 2. _____ 3. _____ 4. _____

B. Phonics

Read the words aloud. Use the phonics skills you have learned.

	A	B	C	D	E	F	G
5.	bore	fir	bind	sold	law	after	perfect
6.	soar	pure	kind	bold	saw	artist	thirsty
7.	core	word	find	cold	taught	dirty	garlic
8.	for	her	wild	hold	caught	disturb	fairway
9.	shore	shirt	child	fold	raw	forty	favor
10.	or	cure	mild	gold	paw	dirty	summer

C. High-Frequency Words

Read the words aloud.

11.	see	number	way	could	people	my
12.	than	first	water	been	call	who

ELPS 2.B recognize elements of the English sound system in newly acquired vocabulary • 3.A practice producing sounds of newly acquired vocabulary • 4.A.1 learn relationships between sounds and letters of the English language • 4.C.1 develop basic sight vocabulary • 5.A learn relationships between sounds and letters when writing in English • 5.C.1 spell familiar English words • 5.C.2 employ English spelling pattern • 5.C.3 employ English spelling rules

NAME _____

D. Listen. Read. Check.

Your teacher will say a word. Mark the box next to the word.

13.	☐ mode		☐ mole		☐ mold
14.	☐ mine		☐ mind		☐ mint
15.	☐ rare		☐ roar		☐ row
16.	☐ pure		☐ peer		☐ pair
17.	☐ roll		☐ ram		☐ raw
18.	☐ tall		☐ talk		☐ told
19.	☐ bur		☐ bird		☐ bear
20.	☐ wild		☐ will		☐ wail

E. Spelling

Your teacher will say a word. Write the word. Check your spelling.

21. _____   23. _____

22. _____   24. _____

ELPS 2.B recognize elements of the English sound system in newly acquired vocabulary • 3.A practice producing sounds of newly acquired vocabulary • 4.A.1 learn relationships between sounds and letters of the English language • 4.C.1 develop basic sight vocabulary • 5.A learn relationships between sounds and letters when writing in English • 5.C.1 spell familiar English words • 5.C.2 employ English spelling pattern • 5.C.3 employ English spelling rules

NAME ————————————————————————————————

CHECKLIST

Word	I've never heard of it.	I've heard of it.	I know what it means.
price	☐	☐	☐
stand	☐	☐	☐
silver	☐	☐	☐
decide	☐	☐	☐
coin	☐	☐	☐
purchase	☐	☐	☐

Which word did you find most challenging?

————————————————————————————————

ELPS 1.C use strategic learning techniques to acquire basic and grade-level vocabulary

NAME _____

CHECKLIST

Word	I've never heard of it.	I've heard of it.	I know what it means.
fortune	☐	☐	☐
increase	☐	☐	☐
treasure	☐	☐	☐
bill	☐	☐	☐
foolish	☐	☐	☐
greed	☐	☐	☐

Which word did you find most interesting?

_____

ELPS 1.C use strategic learning techniques to acquire basic and grade-level vocabulary

NAME —————————————————————————————

READING LONGER WORDS

 You can divide:

- between the words in a compound word.
- after a prefix, or before a suffix.
- between the consonants in a VCCV letter pattern.
- before or after the consonant in a VCV letter pattern.

A. Divide the word. Read each syllable. Then read the whole word.

begin	robot	cubic	music
panic	comic	rapid	robin

B. Divide the word. Read each syllable. Then read the whole word.

reptile	confuse	invite	escape
update	bedtime	online	inside

C. Divide the word. Read each syllable. Then read the whole word.

turnip	target	concert	farther

D. Divide the word. Circle the vowel pair. Read each syllable. Then read the whole word.

elbow	mushroom	shampoo	explain
succeed	window	rainbow	igloo

ELPS 4.A.1 learn relationships between sounds and letters of the English language • 4.A.2 decode words using a combination of skills

141

NAME _____

POEM RUBRIC

When you write a poem, compare it to this rubric. Did you do all you can to make it good?

Poem
A title tells what the poem is about.
Words describe the topic.
Words help readers see, hear, smell, taste, and feel.
The lines in the poem may have a rhythm, or pattern. You can feel or hear this pattern when you read the poem aloud.
The first word in each line in the poem begins with a capital letter.
Grammar, spelling, and punctuation are correct.

ELPS 1.B.2 monitor written language production and employ self-corrective techniques • 4.D use prereading supports to enhance comprehension of written text • 5.G.2 describe with increasing specificity and detail to fulfill content area writing needs

NAME ——

WORD MAP

Poems use descriptive words to help readers picture what they read. The words ask readers to see, hear, smell, taste, and touch. A word map can help you think of words and phrases that describe the subject of a poem. Use this word map to write descriptive words for your poem.

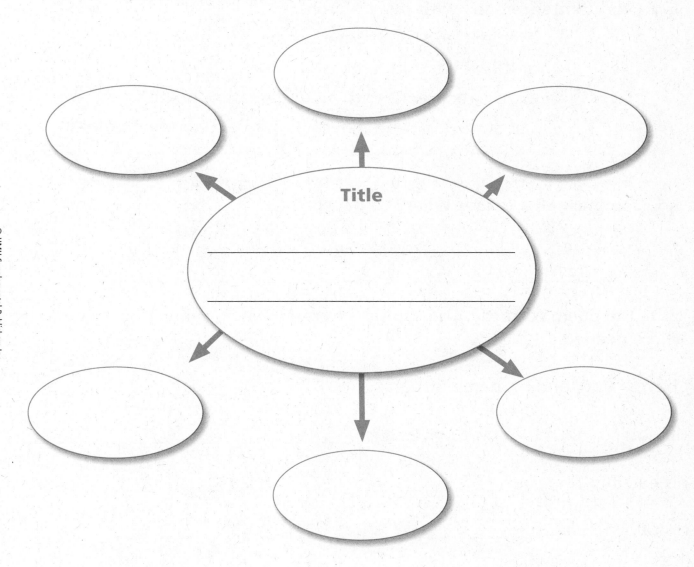

Title

ELPS 4.D use prereading supports to enhance comprehension of written text • 5.G.2 describe with increasing specificity and detail to fulfill content area writing needs

143

NAME _____

CAPITALIZATION AND PUNCTUATION REVIEW

 A sentence always begins with a capital letter.

All proper nouns begin with a capital letter.

The first word in each line of a poem begins with a capital letter.

 Every sentence ends with punctuation.

.	A statement ends with a period.
?	A question ends with a question mark.
!	An exclamation ends with an exclamation point.
. or !	A command ends with a period or an exclamation point.

 Commas tell a reader where to pause.

Use commas to separate three or more items in a list.
The children sang, danced, and acted on the stage.

Write the poem correctly. Use capital letters, commas, and end punctuation where needed.

I have a dog, and his name is rags. _____

He eats so much that his tummy sags. _____

his ears flip-flop, _____

his tail wig-wags, _____

And when he walks, he goes zig-zag _____

NAME _____

EDITING FOR GRAMMAR, SPELLING, AND PUNCTUATION

See also pages 173 and 174.

> The present tense of a verb describes an action that is happening now.
> *The dogs bark.*   *The cat walks.*

> The past tense of a verb describes action that happened in the past.
> *The dogs barked last night.*   *The cat walked away.*

> An adverb describes a verb.
> Incorrect: *The birds sing loud.*
> Correct: *The birds sing loudly.*

Listen to your teacher. Compare the first draft of the poem to the edited draft.

First Draft

Slowly the sun went down,

~slowly~ the shadows grew ∧

Quickly the folks in town

Got ready to eat their stew.

Now the moon shines bright,

Now the night is gray.

Now the people sleep light

And dreamed of the coming day.

Edited Draft

Slowly the sun went down,

Slowly the shadows grew.

Quickly the folks in town

Got ready to eat their stew.

Now the moon shines brightly,

Now the night is gray.

Now the people sleep lightly

And dream of the coming day.

ELPS 5.D.3 edit writing for standard grammar and usage, including appropriate verb tenses • 5.E employ increasingly complex grammatical structures in content area writing

145

NAME _____

READER'S LOG: "MONEY THROUGH THE AGES"

> *i* Active listeners take notes. Active readers do, too. Write only what you need to remember the important information.

PAIR AND SHARE Reread the selection with your partner. Mark the boxes and take notes as you read. Add to your notes as you talk to your partner.

1. How difficult is the selection?
   ☐ very difficult   ☐ not too difficult   ☐ easy

2. What makes the selection difficult?
   ☐ the words   ☐ the information   ☐ everything!

3. List the most difficult words.

   _____

4. What did you do about the difficult words?
   ☐ We talked about them.   ☐ We looked at the pictures.
   ☐ We looked them up in a dictionary.   ☐ We asked our teacher.

5. What did you and your partner already know?
   Me   My partner
   ☐   ☐   a lot about the history of money
   ☐   ☐   something about the history of money
   ☐   ☐   very little—the information was new

6. How did you use the pictures? Did they help you?

   _____

7. Are there any sentences that you don't understand?

   Note the page number, and ask your teacher what they mean. _____

ELPS 2.I.5 demonstrate listening comprehension by taking notes • 4.E read linguistically accommodated content area material • 4.F.6 use support from peers and teachers to read content area text • 4.F.7 use support from peers and teachers to confirm understanding • 4.F.8 use support from peers and teachers to develop vocabulary • 4.F.9 use support from peers and teachers to develop language structures • 4.F.10 use support from peers and teachers to develop background knowledge • 4.G.1 demonstrate comprehension by participating in shared reading • 4.G.4 demonstrate comprehension of English by taking notes

UNIT 8 Vocabulary

NAME —————————————————————————

MATCH IT UP

Write the letter of the definition that matches each word.

1. _____ price   **A** to buy something

2. _____ silver   **B** how much something costs

3. _____ purchase   **C** a small store

4. _____ coin   **D** to think and then make a choice

5. _____ stand   **E** a shiny, gray metal

6. _____ decide   **F** a small piece of metal used as money

NAME _____

USE CLUES

Read each sentence. Use context clues to help you figure out the correct vocabulary word from the box to complete each sentence. Write the word on the line.

treasure	bill	greed	fortune	foolish	increase

1. It would be _____ to go hiking without any water.

_____

2. I had to pay with quarters, because I didn't have a dollar _____.

_____

3. We watched the number of his fans _____ as more people heard his song.

_____

4. The lucky woman discovered _____ hidden in a forgotten cave.

_____

5. I had the good _____ to meet the winner of the race.

_____

6. It was _____ that stopped him from sharing the money he found.

_____

NAME ——————————————————————————————

A. Review

Look at the picture. Read the question. Write the correct answer.

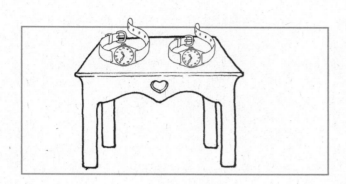

1. Is one watch on the table?

   A Yes, it is.

   B No, two watches are on the table.

   C Yes, I see two watches.

2. Ari wants to make cookies. What is she doing now?

   A She is mixing flour and milk.

   B She has lunch.

   C They mix flour and milk.

3. What is Dad doing?

   A They are riding in the car.

   B It is his car.

   C He is driving his car.

4. What game does Ella play?

   A She plays soccer.

   B They play soccer.

   C She play soccer.

© HMH Supplemental Publishers Inc.

ELPS 4.C.3 comprehend English vocabulary in written classroom materials • 4.C.4 comprehend English language structures in written classroom materials • 4.F.4 use visual and contextual support to develop grasp of language structures

149

NAME _____

B. Which sentence comes next?

Circle the letter of the BEST sentence to follow the sentence or sentences under each picture.

5. This house belongs to Mr. Brown.

   A It is his house.

   B It is her house.

   C It is my house.

6. Look at my dad's books. What if he puts more books on top?

   A They fell.

   B They fall.

   C They will fall.

PAIR AND SHARE With your partner, discuss something that is owned by more than one person.

Use this sentence frame:

A. Ask a question.

   Whose _____ is that? (house, car, bikes)

B. Answer the question.

   That is _____. (my parents' house, my brothers' bikes, my grandparents' car)

Check page 178 to review how to say that more than one person owns something. Be sure to pronounce the *s'*.

Monitor Language: How's your grammar?

Listen to your partner. Was the correct possessive form used? Was the *s'* pronounced?

Yes, always	Sometimes	Never
☐	☐	☐

ELPS 3.C.1 speak using a variety of grammatical structures • 3.C.2 speak using a variety of sentence lengths • 3.C.3 speak using a variety of sentence types • 4.C.3 comprehend English vocabulary in written classroom materials • 4.C.4 comprehend English language structures in written classroom materials • 4.F.4 use visual and contextual support to develop language structures • 4.F.9 use support from peers and teachers to develop language structures

NAME _____

ACTIVE READING OF THE TEXT

 Self-monitor your understanding as you read.

1. **Reread**. Start with the last sentence you understood. Then read on from that point.

2. **Take notes**. Write down the most important details. This can help you understand and remember what you read.

3. **Look up words you don't know.**

4. **Ask questions**. Then look for answers to your questions in the text, or you can ask someone.

From "How to Be a Star"	Active Reading
My first job was picking apples. I had to climb a ladder so that I could reach them. It was hard work, but I made money. I bought myself a new pair of shoes.	Underline anything you do not understand.
	Take notes. What are the most important ideas?
Soon, it was winter. There were no apples left on the trees. I had to get another job. It was the busy holiday season. I worked in a bookstore. With the money I earned, I purchased a new shirt and a tie.	_____ _____ _____
The new year came. So did the snow. I worked clearing the roads. The job didn't last very long, but I earned money. I bought a nice pair of pants.	Tell what you reread or a question you asked. _____ _____ _____

ELPS 4.E read linguistically accommodated content area material • 4.G.4 demonstrate comprehension of English by taking notes

151

NAME _____

READ FOR RATE

Read "Digging Up Money" aloud. Have a partner time your reading for one minute. Then, fill in the chart at the bottom of the page with the number of words you read. Read the passage a second and third time. Try to increase the number of words you read accurately in a minute.

Pirates were driven by greed. They sailed the seas and stole	11
treasure from other ships. The pirate flag showed a skull and	22
bones.	23
When a pirate ship came near, other ships would try to get	35
away. They would be foolish to stay, unless they were ready	46
for a fierce fight. Pirates would show no mercy.	55
What did the pirates do with all their treasure? Sometimes	65
they buried it. Many people have dreamed of finding a	75
pirate's treasure map.	78
If the dream came true, it would be the chance of a lifetime.	91
If you had good fortune, there might be gold hidden	101
underground. It would be the best pay anyone ever got just	112
for digging!	114

Number of Words Read		
First Reading	Second Reading	Third Reading

NAME ———

CHECK YOUR UNDERSTANDING

A. Reread "Money Through the Ages" on **Student Edition** pages 348–357. Then read each sentence below. Circle the letter of the correct answer.

about 10,000 years ago

about 2,500 years ago

about 1,000 years ago

1. A coin is money that is made of _____.

   A metal

   B shell

   C wampum

   D circulatory system

2. The earliest form of money was _____.

   A government bills

   B gold

   C cattle

   D paper money

ELPS 4.E read linguistically accommodated content area material • 4.G.3 demonstrate comprehension by responding to questions

153

NAME _____

B. Read each sentence below. Circle the letter of the correct answer.

3. Before people used money, they _____.

    A used dollars

    B made paper

    C made gold into coins

    D traded one item for another

4. Salt is different from the first paper money because _____.

    A only salt could be traded for gold

    B salt was worth its weight in gold

    C no one was ever paid with salt

    D only paper was ever used money

C. Reread "How to Be a Star" on **Student Edition** pages 358–363. Then read each question below. Circle the letter of the correct answer.

5. What fact do we learn about the person in this selection?

    A He always worked outdoors.

    B He had different jobs as the seasons changed.

    C He saved all his money instead of spending it.

    D He worked as a barber for a while.

6. Why is the selection titled "How to Be a Star"?

    A The selection tells how to get a part in a film.

    B The selection tells a story from a film.

    C The person uses his money to get to Hollywood.

    D The person tells how he became a movie star.

ELPS 4.E read linguistically accommodated content area material • 4.G.3 demonstrate comprehension by responding to questions

NAME _____

A. Label

Write a word that names each picture. Use a word from the word box.

| write | child | lamb | castle | eight | chalk | hulk | walk |

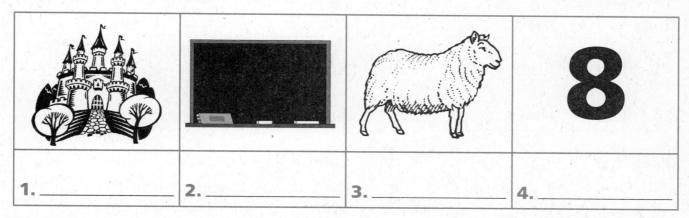

1. _____ 2. _____ 3. _____ 4. _____

B. Phonics

Read these words aloud. Use the phonics skills you have learned.

	A	B	C	D	E	F
5.	talk	high	write	path	photo	tiger
6.	chalk	sight	knit	half	cartoon	hatbox
7.	halt	light	knew	wrap	inside	upset
8.	walk	right	knife	wreck	pupil	supper
9.	salt	might	knee	wrong	raincoat	letter
10.	fault	fight	knock	sign	escape	seesaw

C. High-Frequency Words

Read these words aloud.

| 11. | am | its | now | find | long | down |
| 12. | day | did | get | come | made | part |

ELPS 2.B recognize elements of the English sound system in newly acquired vocabulary • 3.A practice producing sounds of newly acquired vocabulary • 3.B.1 use high-frequency words to identify and describe people, places, and objects • 4.A.1 learn relationships between sounds and letters of the English language • 4.C.1 develop basic sight vocabulary • 5.A learn relationships between sounds and letters when writing in English • 5.C.1 spell familiar English words • 5.C.2 employ English spelling pattern • 5.C.3 employ English spelling rules

NAME _____

D. Listen. Read. Check.

Your teacher will say a word. Mark the box next to the word.

13.	☐ knit		☐ night		☐ nine
14.	☐ road		☐ rot		☐ wrote
15.	☐ night		☐ knife		☐ fine
16.	☐ climb		☐ limb		☐ climate
17.	☐ call		☐ cave		☐ calf
18.	☐ wring		☐ were		☐ rank
19.	☐ hate		☐ eat		☐ eight
20.	☐ shy		☐ sigh		☐ sing

E. Spelling

Write the hardest spelling list you can think of. Then test a friend.

21. _____   23. _____

22. _____   24. _____

ELPS 2.B recognize elements of the English sound system in newly acquired vocabulary • 3.A practice producing sounds of newly acquired vocabulary • 4.A.1 learn relationships between sounds and letters of the English language • 4.C.1 develop basic sight vocabulary • 5.A learn relationships between sounds and letters when writing in English • 5.C.1 spell familiar English words • 5.C.2 employ English spelling pattern • 5.C.3 employ English spelling rules

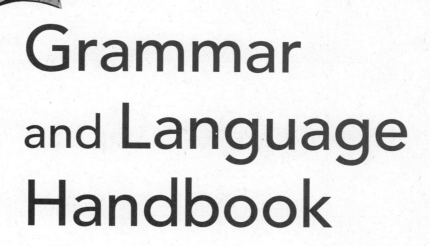

Grammar and Language Handbook

Grammar and Language Handbook

1 What is a noun?

A. A **noun** is a word that names a person, place, or thing.

person	place	thing

boy	park	bus

B. A **noun** can also name an animal.

cat	goat	goldfish

C. A **noun** can name an idea, too.

freedom	happiness	fun

ELPS 3.B.1 use high-frequency words to identify and describe people, places, and objects • 4.F.4 use visual and contextual support to develop grasp of language structures

2 What are singular and plural nouns?

A. A **singular** noun names one person, place, thing, or animal. A **plural** noun names more than one.

To write the plural of many nouns, add -s to the singular noun.

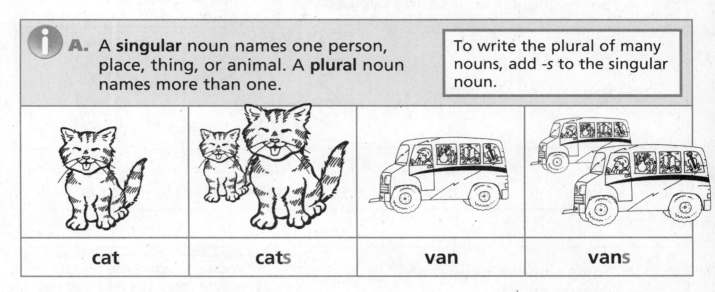

| cat | cats | van | vans |

B. Some **singular** nouns end in *x, ch, tch, sh, zz,* and *ss.*

To write the plural of nouns with these endings, add -es to the singular noun.

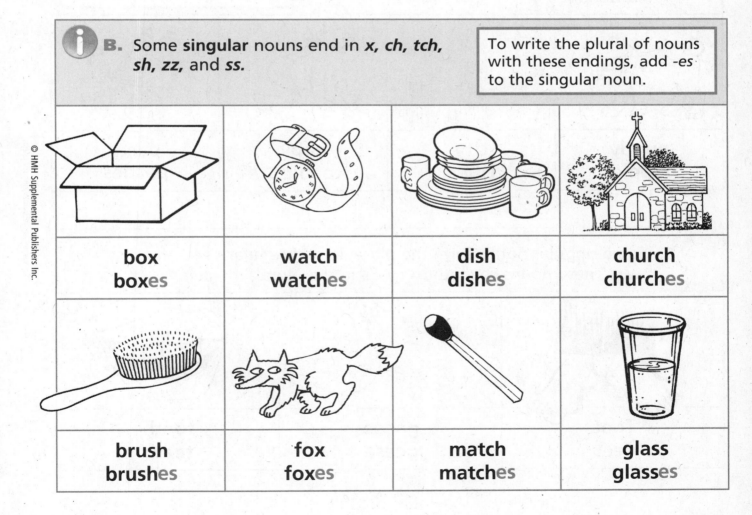

| box
boxes | watch
watches | dish
dishes | church
churches |
| brush
brushes | fox
foxes | match
matches | glass
glasses |

ELPS 4.F.4 use visual and contextual support to develop grasp of language structures

Grammar and Language Handbook

C. Some **singular** nouns end in **vowel + y.**

> If the letter before *y* is a vowel, add *-s* for plural.

key	boy	day	toy
keys	boys	days	toys

D. Some **singular** nouns end in **consonant + y.**

> When you write the plural, change the *y* to *i* and add *-es.*

puppy	city	baby	party
puppies	cities	babies	parties

E. Some singular nouns form the plural in an **irregular** way. These nouns change *oo* to *ee* in the plural.

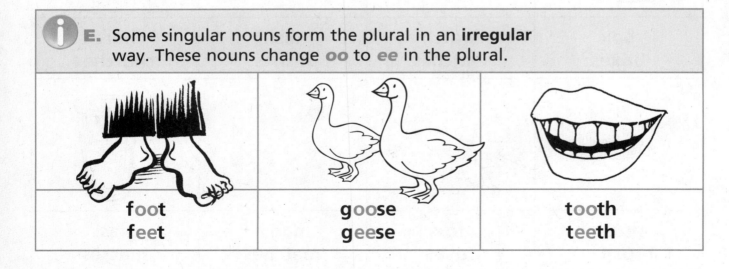

foot	goose	tooth
feet	geese	teeth

ELPS 4.F.4 use visual and contextual support to develop grasp of language structures

F. Some nouns are the same in the singular and the plural. They form the plural in an irregular way.

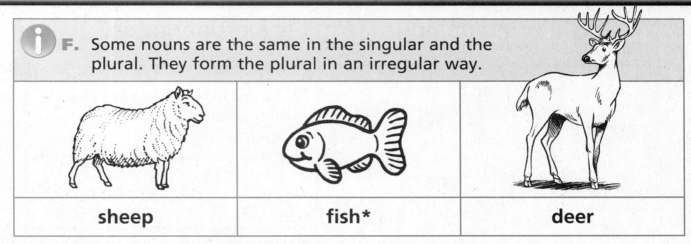

| sheep | fish* | deer |

* The plural of *fish* is sometimes written *fishes*. Both are correct.

G. These nouns name people. The spelling changes in the plural. They form the plural in an irregular way.

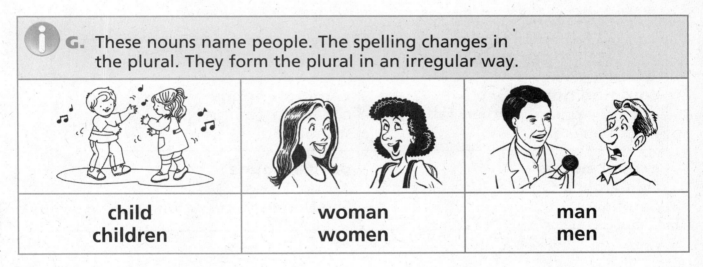

| child
children | woman
women | man
men |

H. These nouns name animals. The spelling changes in the plural. They form the plural in an irregular way.

| mouse
mice | ox
oxen |

Grammar and Language Handbook

3 What is a common noun? What is a proper noun?

A. A **common** noun names any person, place, thing, or animal.

A **proper** noun names a particular person, place, thing, or animal.

Capitalize the **first letter** of the main words in a proper noun.

- Capitalize *the* and *of* only if they are the first words of a proper noun phrase.
- Capitalize **titles**, such as Dr., Ms., Mr., and Mrs.

persons	places
common nouns doctor, woman, mother, father, man, baby, girl	**common nouns** city, state, country, park, school
proper nouns Dr. Carolina Capella, Mrs. Capella, Carolina	**proper nouns** Austin, Texas, The United States of America

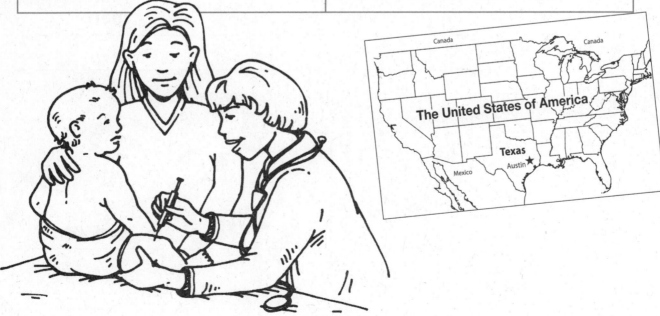

ELPS 4.F.4 use visual and contextual support to develop grasp of language structures

Common and proper nouns

things	animals
common nouns book TV show game	**common nouns** dog cat goat
proper nouns Write the names of your favorite shows or games. **?** _____ _____ _____ _____	**proper nouns** names of pets **Rufus**

B. The words *day* and *month* are common nouns. Specific names of days and months are proper nouns.

Capitalize the days of the week and months of the year.

November

Sunday	Monday	Tuesday	Wednesday	Thursday	Friday	Saturday
			1	2	3	4
5	6	7	8	9	10	11
12	13	14	15	16	17	18
19	20	21	22	23	24	25
26	27	28	29	30		

Grammar and Language Handbook

4 What is an adjective?

 An **adjective** is a word that describes a noun.

- Adjectives give information about nouns. When we read or listen to others speak, adjectives help us picture the nouns.

- When we speak or write, adjectives are words that help us describe what we see, hear, feel, taste, and smell.

huge, big, gray, mammal, male	small, tiny, little, gray, quick	young, spotted, orange and black, female, tall

soft, fluffy, cute, white, young	hard, blue, shiny, metallic	slimy, brown, wiggly, shiny

sweet, pretty, colorful, small	salty, white and yellow, puffy, crunchy	smelly, greasy!

ELPS 4.F.4 use visual and contextual support to develop grasp of language structures

5 What is a definite article?

There is one definite article in English. It is **the**.
Use **the** before any noun when you have only one
thing in mind.

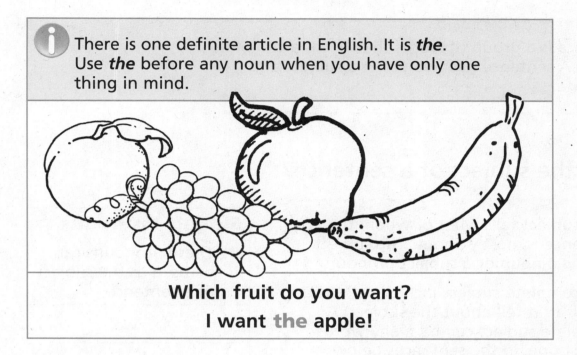

Which fruit do you want?

I want the apple!

6 What are the indefinite articles?

A. There are two indefinite articles: **a** and **an**.

"I want **an** apple!" means "I want **one** apple!"

"I want **a** pear!" means "I want **one** pear!"

You are not definite about which one you want.

B. Use **an** before a word that starts with a vowel.

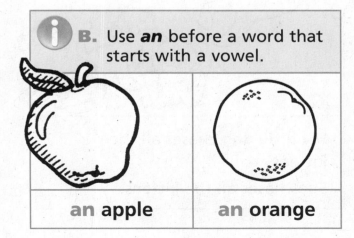

| an apple | an orange |

C. Use **a** before a word that starts with a consonant.

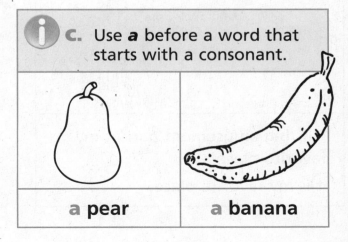

| a pear | a banana |

Grammar and Language Handbook

7 What is a sentence?

A **sentence** is a group of words that forms a complete thought. A sentence has two parts: a **subject** and a **predicate**.

8 What is the subject of a sentence?

A. The **subject** tells what or whom the sentence is mostly about. The subject can be a noun or a subject pronoun.

B. The **complete subject** includes all the words that tell about the subject. A complete subject can be many words or just one. In the sentences below, the complete subject is written in green type.

C. The **simple subject** of a sentence is a noun or a pronoun. In the sentences below, the simple subject is circled.

Subject Pronouns	
D. These pronouns can be used as the subject of a sentence.	
I	we
you	you
he, she, it	they

This big amusement (park) is my favorite place!
(It) is my favorite place.

My little (dog) chases all the kittens.
(She) chases all the kittens.

ELPS 4.F.4 use visual and contextual support to develop grasp of language structures

9 What is the predicate of a sentence?

A. The **predicate** of a sentence includes the main verb and other words that tell more about the verb. The predicate tells what the subject is, does, or feels.

B. The **complete predicate** includes the verb and other words that tell about the verb. In the sentences below, the complete predicate is written in green type.

C. The **simple predicate** is the verb or verb phrase. In the sentences below, the simple predicate is circled.

The girl kicks the ball hard.

The sad little boy is sitting on the floor.

Grammar and Language Handbook

10 What is a sentence fragment?

A **fragment** is a group of words that *do not* form a complete thought! Something important is missing in a sentence fragment.

Read these sentence fragments. What questions do you have when you read them?

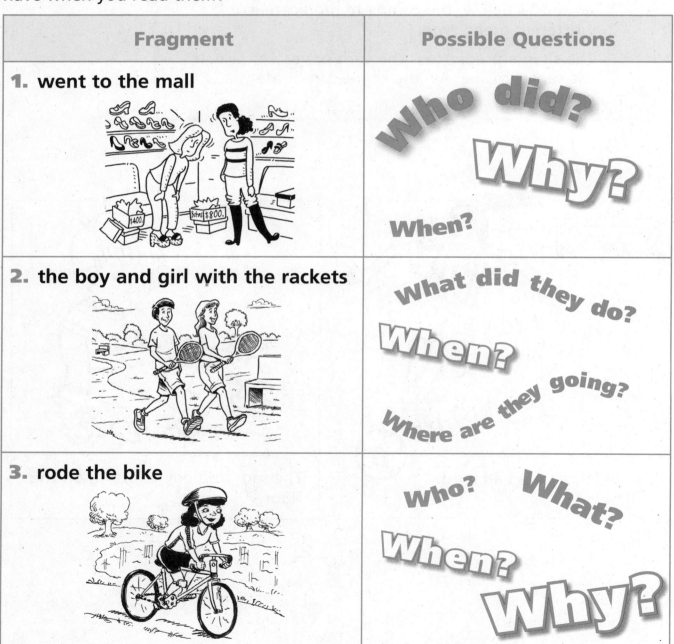

Fragment	Possible Questions
1. went to the mall	Who did? Why? When?
2. the boy and girl with the rackets	What did they do? When? Where are they going?
3. rode the bike	Who? What? When? Why?

ELPS 4.F.4 use visual and contextual support to develop grasp of language structures

11 What are the four kinds of sentences?

ⓘ	Kinds of Sentences	End Punctuation	Intonation
•	**Statement** (or, declarative)	I finished my homework. **(ends with period)**	Your voice should fall at the end of a statement.
?	**Question** (or, interrogative)	Did you finish your homework? **(ends with a question mark)**	Your voice should rise for a question.
!	**Exclamation** (or, exclamatory)	I did it! **(ends with an exclamation mark)**	Your voice should show excitement for an exclamation.
! **or** •	**Command** (or, imperative)	Finish your homework now. (!) **(ends with period or an exclamation mark)**	When you make a command, your voice can vary, depending upon how strongly you feel. Ask your teacher to demonstrate.

Grammar and Language Handbook

12 What forms of the verb *to be* should I use?

 A. Present Tense *to be* Use these verbs to tell about noun and pronoun subjects in the present time.

- Omar **is** tired.
- Those girls **are** good students.

I **am**	We **are**
You **are**	You **are**
He **is** She **is** It **is**	They **are**

B. Past Tense *to be* To tell about the subject of a sentence in the past, use the past tense of *to be*. There are only two verbs to remember!

- Omar **was** tired last night.
- Last year, the girls **were** good students.

I **was**	We **were**
You **were**	You **were**
He **was** She **was** It **was**	They **were**

C. Look at the arrows. Nouns and adjectives can follow forms of the verb *to be*. They always tell about the subject.

Present	Past
Omar **is** tired.	Omar **was** tired last night.
Those girls **are** good students.	The girls **were** good students last year.

ELPS 4.F.4 use visual and contextual support to develop grasp of language structures

13 What contractions are made with *am*, *is*, and *are*?

In English, there is a short, quick way to say some common phrases.

The short form is called a **contraction**.

Contractions can be made with pronoun subjects and present tense forms of the verb *to be*.

PAIR AND SHARE: Speaking
Practice with your partner.
Say the first sentence in each section.
Your partner will respond, using the contraction.
Change roles using the next sentence pairs.
Keep practicing!

A.   I am an athlete.
I'm an athlete.

D.   We are readers.
We're readers.

B.   You are the best!
You're the best!

E.   You are all great.
You're all great.

C.   He is tall.   He's tall.
She is tall.   She's tall.
It is tall.   It's tall.

F.   They are tall.
They're tall.

ELPS 2.E.3 use linguistic support to confirm understanding • 3.C.1 speak using a variety of grammatical structures • 3.C.2 speak using a variety of sentence lengths • 3.C.3 speak using a variety of sentence types • 3.E share information in cooperative learning interactions • 4.F.4 use visual and contextual support to develop grasp of language structures • 4.F.9 use support from peers and teachers to develop grasp of language structures

Grammar and Language Handbook

14 What contractions are made with *not*?

 A. Contractions can be made with the word *not.*
The word *not* makes a sentence negative.

PAIR AND SHARE: Speaking
Practice with your partner.
Say the first sentence in each section.
Your partner will respond, using the contraction.
Change roles using the next sentence pairs.
Keep practicing!

 B. We can form contractions with *not* + **is** and with *not* + **are**.

He is not tall. → He isn't tall.	They are not tall. → They aren't tall.
She is not tall. → She isn't tall.	You are not tall. → You aren't tall.
It is not tall. → It isn't tall.	We are not tall. → We aren't tall.

 C. Contractions can also be made with *not* + **was** and with *not* + **were**.

I was not tall. → I wasn't tall.	We were not tall. → We weren't tall.
He was not tall. → He wasn't tall.	You were not tall. → You weren't tall.
She was not tall. → She wasn't tall.	They were not tall. → They weren't tall.
It was not tall. → It wasn't tall.	

© HMH Supplemental Publishers Inc.

15 What are action verbs?

 A verb is the main word in the predicate of a sentence. An action verb tells what the subject *does*. The verb must agree with the subject. Present tense action verbs have two forms.

PAIR AND SHARE: Speaking

Practice reading the sentences below the illustrations with your partner.

Pronounce the *-s* or *-es* endings in the verbs very clearly.

Your partner should be able to hear the ending in these verbs.

Then change roles.

Agreement Rules for Present Tense Action Verbs

Rule 1 Add *-s* to most present tense action verbs if the subject is a singular noun or a singular subject pronoun: *he, she, it.*	**Rule 2** Add *-es* to the present tense verb if it ends in *-ch, -tch, -sh, -ss, -x,* or *-zz* and the subject is a singular noun or a singular subject pronoun: *he, she, it.*

Four players **run** to the ball. Julio **gets** there first! He **kicks** the ball. His team **wins**.	The runners **dash** to the finish line. Marta **catches** up. She **passes** them all. She **finishes** first.

ELPS 2.E.3 use linguistic support to confirm understanding • 3.C.1 speak using a variety of grammatical structures • 3.C.2 speak using a variety of sentence lengths • 3.C.3 speak using a variety of sentence types • 3.E share information in cooperative learning interactions • 4.F.4 use visual and contextual support to develop grasp of language structures • 4.F.9 use support from peers and teachers to develop grasp of language structures

© HMH Supplemental Publishers Inc.

Grammar and Language Handbook

16 What is the correct form of regular action verbs in the past tense?

 In English, the same form is used for all regular past tense verbs.

- When you write, add **-ed** to the verb to form the past tense.

- When you speak, be sure to pronounce the **-ed** ending.

Singular Subject
I work**ed** last night.
John, you work**ed** last night.
The boy work**ed** last night. The girl work**ed** last night. The car work**ed** last night. He, she, and it work**ed** last night.

Plural Subject
We work**ed** last night.
John and Darcy, you both work**ed** last night.
The students work**ed** last night. The dogs work**ed** last night. The cars work**ed** last night. They work**ed** last night.

17 What are common irregular action verbs?

A. The verbs *go, do,* and *have* are irregular in the present tense. They are called *irregular* because we don't *just* add *s* when the subject is a singular noun or *he, she, it.*

B. The verbs *go, do,* and *have* are also irregular in the past tense. The same form is used for all subjects.

Present Tense			
Pronoun Subjects	**Verb**		
	go	**do**	**have**
I, You, We, They	go	do	have
He, She, It	goes	does	has

Past Tense	
to go	went
to do	did
to have	had

Verb *go*	Verb *do*	Verb *have*
We go home after school. Kim goes home after school. Kim went home after school yesterday.	We do our homework. He does his homework on time. He did his homework on time last week.	We have a lot of books. The man has a lot of books. The man had a lot of books before he moved.

Grammar and Language Handbook

18 What are direct objects?

A.
- **Nouns** that are **direct objects** are affected by the verb.
- To find the direct object in a sentence, say the verb. Then ask, **What?** or **Whom?**

B. **Direct object pronouns** can replace nouns in a sentence. When you replace a noun that is a direct object, use *them* if the noun is plural. If the noun is singular, use *him, her,* or *it*.

Singular	Plural
me	us
you	you
him, her, it	them

1. My friends feed the ducks.
   Feed *what*? the ducks
   The direct object is ducks.

2. My friends feed them.
   The direct object is them.

3. The player kicks the ball.
   Kicks *what*? the ball
   The direct object is ball.

4. The player kicks it.
   The direct object is it.

ELPS 4.F.4 use visual and contextual support to develop grasp of language structures

19 How do we show possession or ownership?

A. English has a special way to show that one person owns something. Use apostrophes!

This cat belongs to Sumi.

This cat is Sumi's.

This is Sumi's cat.

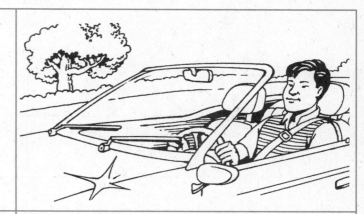

The car belongs to my dad.

The car is my dad's.

It is my dad's car.

B. **When you write,** here's how to show that one person owns something.

When you speak, be sure to pronounce the **s** that follows the apostrophe.

Step 1	Write the noun that names the person.	Sumi	Dad
Step 2	Write an *apostrophe s* after the noun.	Sumi's	Dad's
Step 3	Write what is owned.	Sumi's cat	Dad's car

Grammar and Language Handbook

© HMH Supplemental Publishers Inc.

 C. Here's how to show that more than one person owns something.

The bike belongs to the boys.
This is the **boys'** bike.

These hoops belong to my sisters.
They are my **sisters'** hoops.

 D. **When you write,** here's how to show that more than one person owns something.

When you speak, be sure to pronounce the *s* ending of the plural noun.

Step 1	Write the noun phrase that names the persons who own something.	the two boys	my sisters
Step 2	Write an *apostrophe* after the plural noun.	the two boys'	my sisters'
Step 3	Write what is owned.	the two boys' bike	my sisters' hoops

E. You can replace possessive nouns with possessive pronouns.

- Some possessive pronouns come before the noun.

- Some possessive pronouns are not followed by a noun.

other possessive pronouns	
before a noun	**alone**
my bike	mine
your cat	yours
our car	ours

This is the **boys'** bike.
This is **their** bike.
The bike is **theirs**.

They are my **sisters'** hoops.
They are **their** hoops.
The hoops are **theirs**.

This is **Sumi's** cat.
This is **her** cat.
This cat is **hers**.

This is my **dad's** car.
This is **his** car.
This car is **his**.

20 How do we show that something is happening right now?

A. Here are two ways to talk about actions that are happening in the present tense.

B. Use the simple present tense when actions occur regularly or often.	**C.** To show that something is happening right now, use the correct form of **to be** + the **ing** form of the action verb.
Simple Present	**Present Progressive**
1. I **read** every day.	I **am reading** right now.*
2. The girls **sing** a lot.	The girls **are singing** right now.*
3. Celeste always **studies** math.	Celeste **is studying** math right now.*

*In these sentences, *am, are* and *is* are helping verbs.

21 How do we show that an action will happen in the future?

> **A.** In English, there is an easy way to show that an action will happen in the future. The magic word is *will.* Just write *will* plus the main verb.

Present Tense	Future Tense
1. I am studying hard now.	I will go to a great college.
2. You are a good student now.	You will be a good doctor.
3. He is not watching television now.	He will watch tonight.

> **B.** You can form a contraction with subject pronouns and *will.*

I will ➝ I'll	We will ➝ we'll	He will ➝ he'll

> **C.** To say that something will **not** happen in the future, you can use **will not** or **won't**.
>
> *Won't* means the opposite of *will.* You can say either:
>
> I *will not* go to bed or I *won't* go to bed.

Grammar and Language Handbook

22 What are negative words in English?

PAIR AND SHARE: Speaking
Study this page with your partner. Then close the book. See how many negative words you can list! Then practice saying a sentence, using just one negative word! Try some alternatives with the positive word list.

A. In formal English, use only one negative word in a sentence.

B. What are the negative words?

no	not	never	nobody	nothing	nowhere
isn't	wasn't	weren't	don't	doesn't	won't

C. If you already have one negative in a sentence, you can use *positive* words that are the opposite of the *negative* words.

negative words	never	nobody	nothing	nowhere
positive words	always	somebody anybody	something anything	somewhere anywhere

Not This	Try This
1. I never talk to nobody in class!	I never talk to anybody in class. I talk to nobody in class.
2. I didn't do nothing!	I didn't do anything. I did nothing.
3. I won't go nowhere today!	I won't go anywhere today. I will go nowhere today.

ELPS 2.E.3 use linguistic support to confirm understanding • 3.E share information in cooperative learning interactions • 4.F.4 use visual and contextual support to develop grasp of language structures • 4.F.9 use support from peers and teachers to develop grasp of language structures

23 How can we make our sentences interesting?

> When you write, try making some sentences short. Make some sentences long. Change the way your sentences begin. There are many ways to vary your sentences.

Strategy 1. You can use the **connecting** word *and* to combine different subjects when you write or speak. Be sure to use a plural verb if the subject in the new sentence is plural.

1. A watch is on the table.

2. A cell phone is on the table.

Write or say: A watch and a cell phone are on the table.

PAIR AND SHARE: Speaking

Find two objects in the same location (under a desk, on the wall).

Say where one object is in a sentence.

Describe where the second object is.

Combine the sentences using *and*.

Use Strategy 1 as the model.

ELPS 2.E.3 use linguistic support to confirm understanding • 3.C.1 speak using a variety of grammatical structures • 3.C.2 speak using a variety of sentence lengths • 3.C.3 speak using a variety of sentence types • 3.C.4 speak using a variety of connecting words • 3.E share information in cooperative learning interactions • 4.F.4 use visual and contextual support to develop grasp of language structures • 4.F.9 use support from peers and teachers to develop grasp of language structures

PAIR AND SHARE: Speaking
Name one thing you like in a sentence.
Name one thing you don't like in another sentence.
Combine the sentences using *but*.
Use Strategy 2 as the model.

Strategy 2. When the subject in two sentences is the same, look for differences. If only one sentence has the word *not*, you may be able to combine sentences using the connecting word *but*.

1. I like the watch.

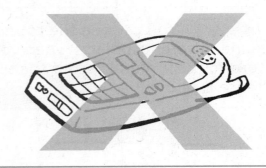

2. I do not like the cell phone.

Write or say: I like the watch, but not the cell phone.

Strategy 3. Combine subjects that are different using a pronoun to replace the noun subjects.

1. My parents are good cooks.
(This is a simple subject.)

2. I am a good cook.
(This is a simple subject.)

Write or say: My parents and I are good cooks. (This is a compound subject.)
We are good cooks. (This is a simple subject.)

ELPS 2.E.3 use linguistic support to confirm understanding • 3.C.1 speak using a variety of grammatical structures • 3.C.2 speak using a variety of sentence lengths • 3.C.3 speak using a variety of sentence types • 3.C.4 speak using a variety of connecting words • 3.E share information in cooperative learning interactions • 4.F.4 use visual and contextual support to develop grasp of language structures • 4.F.9 use support from peers and teachers to develop grasp of language structures

Strategy 4. Use these pairs of conjunctions to combine sentences.

either or
neither nor

1. I will not scold my dog.

2. I will not scold my cat.

Write or say: I will not scold **either** my dog **or** my cat.
Or... I will scold **neither** my dog **nor** my cat.

Strategy 5. Some verb forms can be used as adjectives. Look for verb forms ending in *-ed* or *-ing*. See if there are ways to combine sentences using these verb forms.

Buzz! Buzz! Buzz!

1. The bees are buzzing.

2. The bees landed on a flower.

Write or say: The **buzzing** bees landed on a flower.

ELPS 2.E.3 use linguistic support to confirm understanding • 3.C.1 speak using a variety of grammatical structures • 3.C.2 speak using a variety of sentence lengths • 3.C.3 speak using a variety of sentence types • 3.C.4 speak using a variety of connecting words • 3.E share information in cooperative learning interactions • 4.F.9 use support from peers and teachers to develop grasp of language structures

Grammar and Language Handbook

Strategy 6. Sometimes it is possible to combine sentences using one of these conjunctions.

after	before	because	when	until

When you combine two sentences using these conjunctions, you often need a comma to separate the two parts of the new sentence.

1. First I eat breakfast.

2. Then I get dressed.

Write or say: **After** eating breakfast, I get dressed.
Or...   **Before** getting dressed, I eat breakfast.

PAIR AND SHARE: Speaking

Think of two things you do in a certain order.

Write a sentence about each one. (Use words such as *first, next,* and *then* to show the order.)

Combine the two sentences using conjunctions such as *after, before, because, when, until.*

Use Strategy 6 as the model.

ELPS 2.E.3 use linguistic support to confirm understanding • 3.C.1 speak using a variety of grammatical structures • 3.C.2 speak using a variety of sentence lengths • 3.C.3 speak using a variety of sentence types • 3.C.4 speak using a variety of connecting words • 3.E share information in cooperative learning interactions • 4.F.4 use visual and contextual support to develop grasp of language structures • 4.F.9 use support from peers and teachers to develop grasp of language structures

Phonics
and Spelling
Handbook

Phonics and Spelling Handbook

Consonant Letters and Sounds

What is a Consonant?

A consonant is a letter and a speech sound. Consonant sounds are made when some part of the mouth blocks the air when you speak. Your lips, teeth, and tongue can block the air.

PAIR and SHARE: Phonics

Learn a key word that begins with each consonant letter. For example, the letter *f* stands for the sound at the beginning of *fish*.

Use the key word to remind you of the sound this letter stands for.

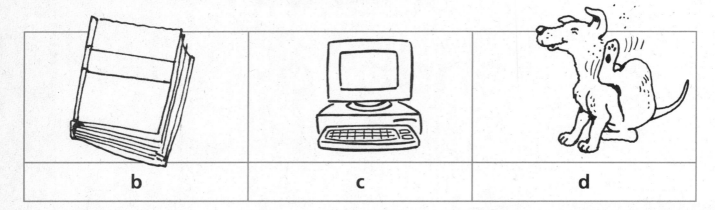

| b | c | d |

| f | g | h |

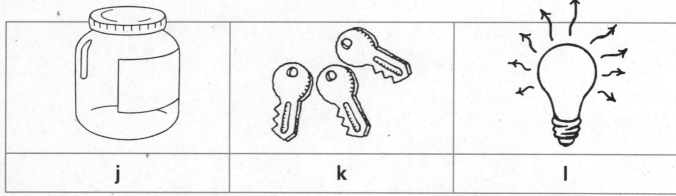

| j | k | l |

ELPS 3.E share information in cooperative learning interactions • 4.A.1 learn relationships between sounds and letters of the English language

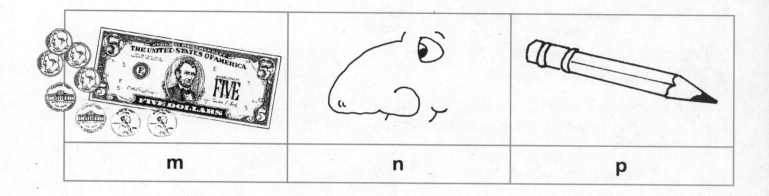

m	**n**	**p**

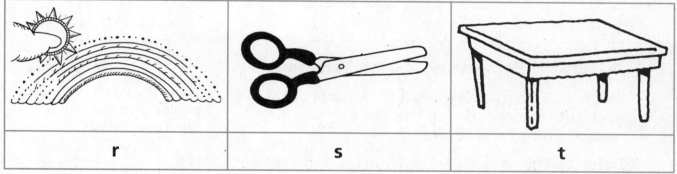

r	**s**	**t**

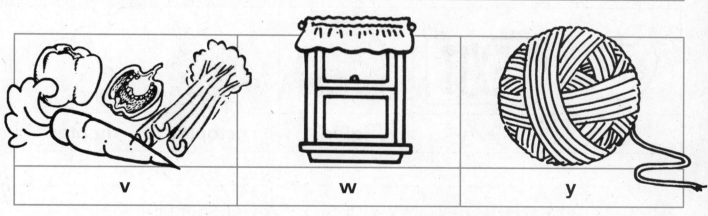

v	**w**	**y**

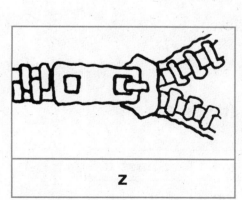

z

PAIR AND SHARE: Spelling

Say a new word aloud.

Match the first sounds in the new word and your key word.

Write the letter.

ELPS 3.E share information in cooperative learning interactions • 4.A.1 learn relationships between sounds and letters of the English language

189

Phonics and Spelling Handbook

Vowel Letters and Sounds

 A. What is a Vowel?

- A vowel is a letter and is a speech sound. Vowel sounds are made when air is *not* blocked by some part of the mouth.

- There are five vowel letters: *a, e, i, o, u.*

- In English, all vowel letters stand for more than one sound.

 B. How to Remember Short Vowel Sounds

PHONICS Learn a key word that starts with each short vowel sound. Use the key word to remind you of the sound.

Listen to the first sound as your teacher says each word.

PAIR and SHARE
Say, "Short a" (or e, i, o, u). Your partner will name the key word that begins with the sound. Then change roles.

apple	exit	igloo	octopus	umbrella

 C. Letter Patterns in Words with Short Vowel Sounds

PHONICS Look at the word. Answer these questions:

1. Does the word have just one vowel letter?

2. Does the word end in a consonant letter?

If you can answer *yes,* the vowel letter probably stands for a short vowel sound.

Short a	Short e	Short i	Short o	Short u
an, man	Ed, bed	in, pin	on, mop	up, cup

ELPS 2.B recognize elements of the English sound system in newly acquired vocabulary • 3.A practice producing sounds of newly acquired vocabulary • 3.E share information in cooperative learning interactions • 4.A.1 learn relationships between sounds and letters of the English language

Words with Short Vowels Sounds

 PHONICS Reading

Read the slow way. Point to each letter.
Say the sound.

Read the fast way. Say the whole word.

Circle a word if you have trouble reading it.

Ask your teacher for help if you need it.

Words with Short *a*

c a n ➔ **can**	b a g ➔ **bag**	r a m ➔ **ram**	v a n ➔ **van**

Words with Short *e*

j e t ➔ **jet**	h e n ➔ **hen**	l e g ➔ **leg**	w e t ➔ **wet**

ELPS 2.B recognize elements of the English sound system in newly acquired vocabulary • 3.A practice producing sounds of newly acquired vocabulary • 4.A.1 learn relationships between sounds and letters of the English language • 4.A.2 decode words using a combination of skills

191

Phonics and Spelling Handbook

Words with Short *i*

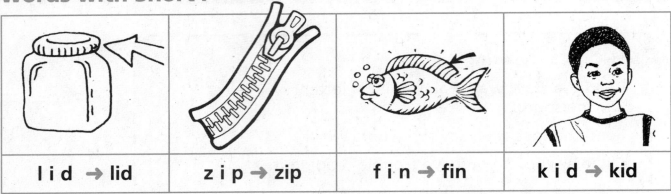

| l i d → lid | z i p → zip | f i n → fin | k i d → kid |

Words with Short *o*

| d o t → dot | m o p → mop | p o t → pot | t o p → top |

Words with Short *u*

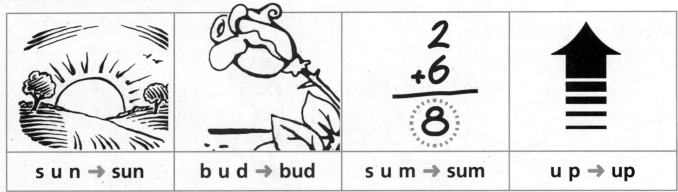

| s u n → sun | b u d → bud | s u m → sum | u p → up |

PAIR AND SHARE: Spelling
Say the word aloud.
Say each sound as your partner writes each letter.
Change roles. It's your turn to write a word.
Circle hard words.

ELPS 2.B recognize elements of the English sound system in newly acquired vocabulary • 3.A practice producing sounds of newly acquired vocabulary • 3.E share information in cooperative learning interactions • 4.A.1 learn relationships between sounds and letters of the English language • 4.A.2 decode words using a combination of skills

Special Consonants

 A. The Letter x

The letter *x* stands for more than one sound.
Listen as your teacher reads these words.

	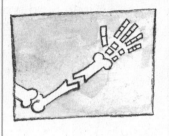		
xylophone	**x-ray**	**six**	**exit**

 B. Where x Appears

The letter *x* appears most often at the end of a word or syllable.

Circle the *x* in these words. The letter *x* stands for two sounds: /k/ and /s/. Listen as your teacher reads the words.

PAIR and SHARE: Phonics
Read each word.
Remember: The letter *x* stands for two sounds!
Listen to your partner read.
Circle hard words.

			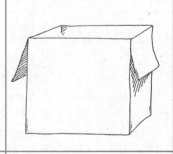	
fox	**mix**		**box**	**sax**

ELPS 3.A practice producing sounds of newly acquired vocabulary • 3.E share information in cooperative learning interactions • 4.A.1 learn relationships between sounds and letters of the English language • 4.A.2 decode words using a combination of skills

193

Phonics and Spelling Handbook

 C. Letters *ck*

The letters *ck* stand for one sound. You will find them at the end of a word or syllable. Listen as your teacher reads the words.

PAIR and SHARE: Phonics
Underline *ck* and *qu* in each word.
Read each word.
Listen to your partner read.
Circle hard words.

duck	**pack**	**sock**	**kick**

 D. Letters *qu*

The letter *q* does not like to be alone! When you see a *q*, look for *u*! Together these letters stand for two sounds: /k/ + /w/. Listen as your teacher reads the words. Repeat.

queen	**quit**	**quack**	**quiet**

"QUIET, DUCK!" SAID THE QUEEN.
"QUIT QUACKING!"

PAIR AND SHARE: Spelling final *x*, *ck*, **and initial** *qu*

Say the word aloud.

Say each sound as your partner writes each letter or letters.

Remember:
- At the end of a word, the sound /k/ is usually written with two letters: *ck*.
- The two sounds /k/ and /w/ together are often written with the letters *qu*.
- When you hear the sounds /k/ /s/ at the end of a word, they may be spelled with an *x*.

Change roles. It's your turn to write a word.

Circle hard words.

© HMH Supplemental Publishers Inc.

ELPS 3.A practice producing sounds of newly acquired vocabulary • 3.E share information in cooperative learning interactions • 4.A.1 learn relationships between sounds and letters of the English language • 4.A.2 decode words using a combination of skills

E. Double Consonant Letters

Sometimes, words or syllables end in double consonants. The two letters always stand for one consonant sound.

PAIR and SHARE: Reading
Read the word.
Listen to your partner read.
Circle hard words.

			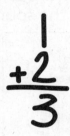
egg	**kiss**	**bell**	**add**

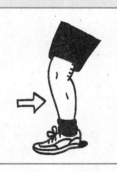

F. Spelling Alert

Read the words above one more time. Many words ending in these sounds are spelled with a single consonant letter. Read the words below. Make sure you know whether the final consonant letter is doubled when you write the word.

l e g → leg	**b u s → bus**	**p a l → pal**	**d a d → dad**

ELPS 3.A practice producing sounds of newly acquired vocabulary • 3.E share information in cooperative learning interactions • 4.A.1 learn relationships between sounds and letters of the English language • 4.A.2 decode words using a combination of skills

195

Phonics and Spelling Handbook

Words with Long Vowel Sounds

 A. PHONICS Do you know the name of each vowel letter? That is important information because long vowels say their own names. Your teacher will show you what that means.

Learn a key word that starts with each long vowel sound. Use the key word to remind you of the sound this letter stands for.

		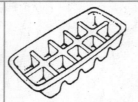		
long *a* in **apron**	long *e* in **eat**	long *i* in **ice**	long *o* in **ocean**	Long *u* in **united**

 B. Letter Pattern: consonant + vowel (as in *me, be, see*)

PHONICS When a vowel letter is at the end of a word or syllable, it usually has a *long* vowel sound. The letter *y* has the same sound as long *i* at the end of a word.

PAIR and SHARE. Read each word. Circle words that are difficult. Practice spelling the word.

Vowel Letters	Words with Long Vowel Sounds
e or *ee*	be he me we bee see Lee
i or *y*	hi by my
o	no so go

 C. Irregular Words: *do* and *to*

These words *don't* have a long vowel sound! They are irregular. Listen as your teacher reads them.

ELPS 2.B recognize elements of the English sound system in newly acquired vocabulary • 3.A practice producing sounds of newly acquired vocabulary • 3.E share information in cooperative learning interactions • 4.A.1 learn relationships between sounds and letters of the English language • 4.A.2 decode words using a combination of skills • 4.C.1 develop basic sight vocabulary

Vowel Pairs with Long Vowel Sounds

A. Vowel pairs: *ee* and *ea*

PHONICS The vowel letters *ee* stand for the long e sound. In most words, the two letters *ea* also stand for the long e *sound*. Circle the vowel pair in each word. Remember, the two vowel letters stand for one vowel sound. Listen as your teacher reads each word.

PAIR and SHARE:
Reading
Read the word.
Listen to your partner read.
Circle hard words.

| beet | meal | peel |

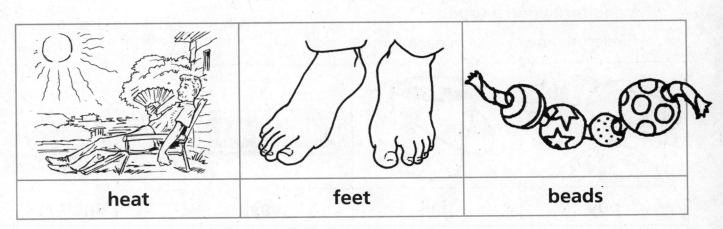

| heat | feet | beads |

ELPS 2.B recognize elements of the English sound system in newly acquired vocabulary • 3.A practice producing sounds of newly acquired vocabulary • 3.E share information in cooperative learning interactions • 4.A.1 learn relationships between sounds and letters of the English language • 4.A.2 decode words using a combination of skills

Phonics and Spelling Handbook

Vowel Pairs with Long Vowel Sounds

 B. Vowel pair *oa*

PHONICS The vowel letters *oa* stand for the long *o* sound in most words. Underline the vowel pair in each word. Remember, the two vowel letters stand for one vowel sound. Listen as your teacher reads each word.

PAIR and SHARE: Reading
Read the word.
Listen to your partner read.
Circle hard words.

boat

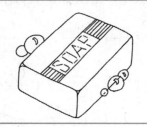

toad

soap

oak

 C. Vowel pairs *ai* and *ay*

PHONICS The vowel pairs *ai* and *ay* stand for a long *a* sound.

Circle the vowel pair in each word.

SPELLING NOTE:
• *ay* is found at the end of a word.
• *ai* is found at the beginning or in the middle of a word.

pay

pail

way

rain

PAIR and SHARE: Spelling
Long vowel sounds can be spelled in different ways. If you are not sure of the spelling of a word, look it up in a dictionary. Practice spelling the words on this page with your partner.

ELPS 2.B recognize elements of the English sound system in newly acquired vocabulary • 3.A practice producing sounds of newly acquired vocabulary • 3.E share information in cooperative learning interactions • 4.A.1 learn relationships between sounds and letters of the English language • 4.A.2 decode words using a combination of skills

Long Vowel Letter Pattern: VCe

A. Letter pattern: vowel + consonant + e

PHONICS Look for this letter pattern:
Vowel + Consonant + e

1. The first vowel is long.

2. The final e is silent.

Listen as your teacher reads these words.

c a p e   p i n e   n o t e   c u b e   P e t e

SPELLING NOTE:
Words with long vowel sounds that end in a consonant can be spelled in several ways. Look up words with these patterns if you are unsure of the spelling.

long *a*	long *i*	long *o*	long *u*	long *e*
c a p e	p i n e	n o t e	c u b e	P e t e

B. READING STRATEGY

1. Does the word end in e? **Circle it.**

2. Does a consonant letter precede the final e? **Check.**

3. Does a vowel letter precede the consonant? **Underline it.**

4. Read the word:

   • The first vowel is long.

   • The final e is silent.

ELPS 2.B recognize elements of the English sound system in newly acquired vocabulary • 3.A practice producing sounds of newly acquired vocabulary • 3.E share information in cooperative learning interactions • 4.A.1 learn relationships between sounds and letters of the English language • 4.A.2 decode words using a combination of skills

Phonics and Spelling Handbook

Long Vowel Letter Pattern: VCe

PAIR and SHARE:
Phonics
Use the reading strategy to read these words.

C. Long *a* spelled Vowel + Consonant + *e*

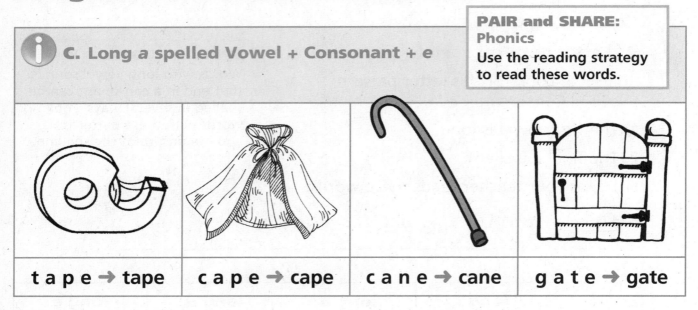

t a p e → tape | c a p e → cape | c a n e → cane | g a t e → gate

D. Long *e* spelled Vowel + Consonant + *e*

Most words with long e vowels with this letter pattern are people's names.

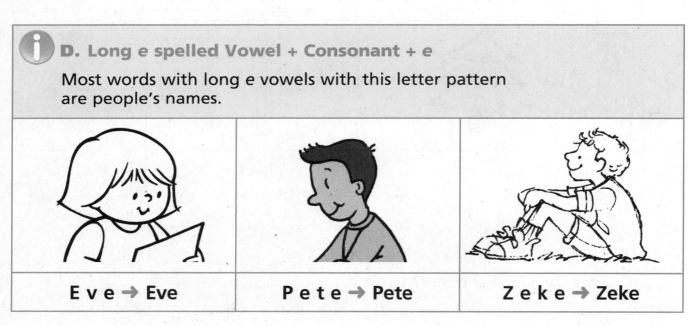

E v e → Eve | P e t e → Pete | Z e k e → Zeke

PAIR and SHARE: Spelling
Long vowel sounds can be spelled in different ways. If you are not sure of the spelling of a word, look it up in a dictionary. Practice spelling the words on this page with your partner.

© HMH Supplemental Publishers Inc.

PAIR and SHARE:
Phonics
Use the reading strategy
to read these words.

E. Long *i* spelled Vowel + Consonant + e

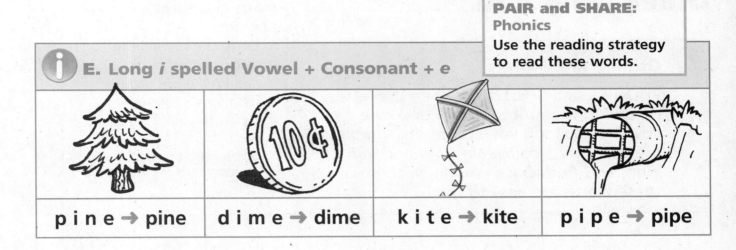

| p i n e → pine | d i m e → dime | k i t e → kite | p i p e → pipe |

F. Long *o* spelled Vowel + Consonant + e

| b o n e → bone | c o n e → cone | n o t e → note | r o p e → rope |

G. Long *u* spelled Vowel + Consonant + e

The long *u* has two sounds: the sound you hear in *cube* and the sound you hear in *tube*.

SPELLING NOTE:
When you are writing a word with either of the two long *u* sounds plus a final consonant, use a VCe letter pattern.

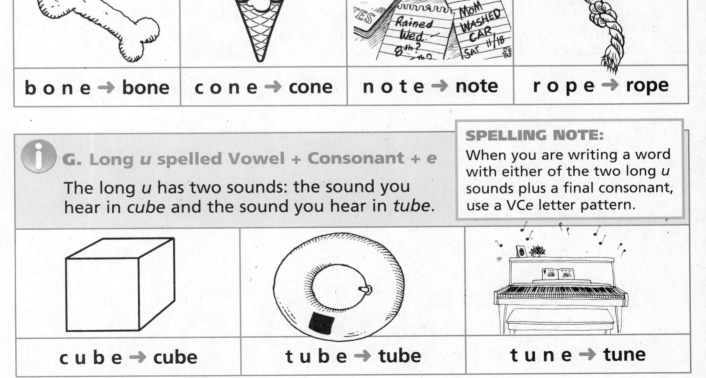

| c u b e → cube | t u b e → tube | t u n e → tune |

PAIR and SHARE: Spelling
Long vowel sounds can be spelled in different ways. If you are not sure of the spelling of a word, look it up in a dictionary. Practice spelling the words on this page with your partner.

ELPS 2.B recognize elements of the English sound system in newly acquired vocabulary • 3.A practice producing sounds of newly acquired vocabulary • 3.E share information in cooperative learning interactions • 4.A.1 learn relationships between sounds and letters of the English language • 4.A.2 decode words using a combination of skills

201

Other Long Vowels

 Other Long Vowels

PHONICS and SPELLING When the letters *nd* and *ld* are preceded by *i* or *o*, the vowel has a long vowel sound. Examples are *wild, mild, cold, sold, told* and *mind, kind,* and *find*. Once you know the rule, these words are easy to spell.

PAIR and SHARE:
Phonics
1. **Circle** the vowel letter.
2. **Underline** *nd* or *ld*.
3. **Read** the word using a long vowel sound.
4. **Listen** to your partner read.
5. **Circle** hard words.

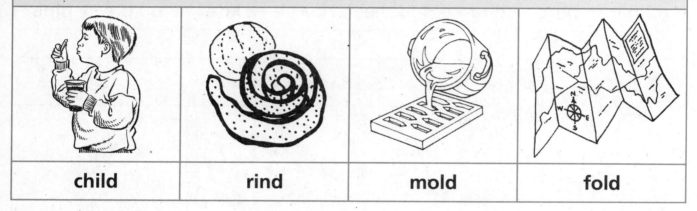

| child | rind | mold | fold |

ELPS 2.B recognize elements of the English sound system in newly acquired vocabulary • 3.A practice producing sounds of newly acquired vocabulary • 3.E share information in cooperative learning interactions • 4.A.1 learn relationships between sounds and letters of the English language • 4.A.2 decode words using a combination of skills

Two Sounds of *c* and *g*

PAIR and SHARE: Phonics
1. **Circle** the letter *c* or *g*.
2. **Underline** the letter that follows *c* or *g*.
3. **Read** the word.
4. **Listen** to your partner read.
5. **Circle** hard words.

PHONICS NOTES about *c* and *g*

Hard *c* and *g* The letter *c* stands for the sound at the beginning of *computer*. The letter *g* stands for the sound at the beginning of *gate*.

These sounds are called *hard c* and *hard g* sounds.

Soft *c* and *g* When the letters *c* and *g* are followed by *i*, *e*, or *y*, they usually stand for other sounds. Listen as your teacher reads the words below. The letters *c* and *g* are called *soft c* and *g* sounds in these words.

Soft C

mice	face	cent	city

Soft G

cage	page	gem	gym

PAIR and SHARE: Spelling

Be careful!

• Soft *c* as in *cent* can also be spelled with the letter *s*, as in *sent*.

• Soft *g* as in *gem* can also be spelled with the letter *j*, as in *jet*.

If you are unsure of the spelling, look up the word in a dictionary.

ELPS 2.B recognize elements of the English sound system in newly acquired vocabulary • 3.A practice producing sounds of newly acquired vocabulary • 4.A.1 learn relationships between sounds and letters of the English language • 4.A.2 decode words using a combination of skills

© HMH Supplemental Publishers Inc.

Consonant Digraphs and Trigraphs

 A. Digraphs and Trigraphs *ch, tch, ph, sh, th,* and *wh*

PHONICS These consonant letters stand for just one sound.

PAIR and SHARE: Phonics
Underline the digraph or trigraph.
Read each word.
Listen to your partner read.
Circle hard words.

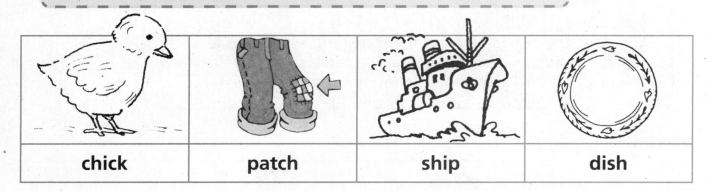

| chick | patch | ship | dish |

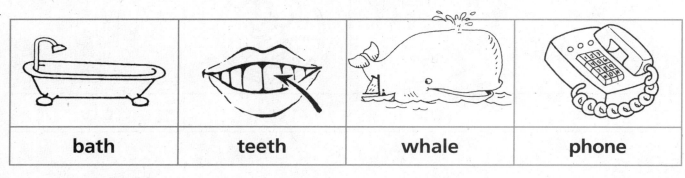

| bath | teeth | whale | phone |

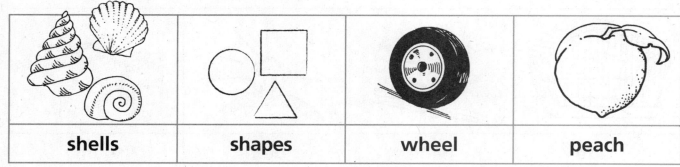

| shells | shapes | wheel | peach |

PAIR and SHARE: Spelling
The sound /ch/ is spelled in two ways: *ch* and *tch*. The spelling *tch* is found only at the end of a word, and *ch* is found at the beginning and end (as in *church*).

© HMH Supplemental Publishers Inc.

ELPS 2.B recognize elements of the English sound system in newly acquired vocabulary • 3.A practice producing sounds of newly acquired vocabulary • 3.E share information in cooperative learning interactions • 4.A.1 learn relationships between sounds and letters of the English language • 4.A.2 decode words using a combination of skills

ⓘ **B. Digraphs *ng* and *nk***

PHONICS Two other consonant pairs stand for one sound. Listen as your teacher reads the words below.

PAIR and SHARE: Phonics
Underline the digraph.
Read each word.
Listen to your partner read.
Circle hard words.

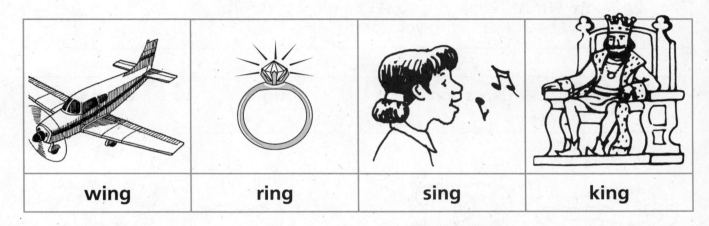

wing   ring   sing   king

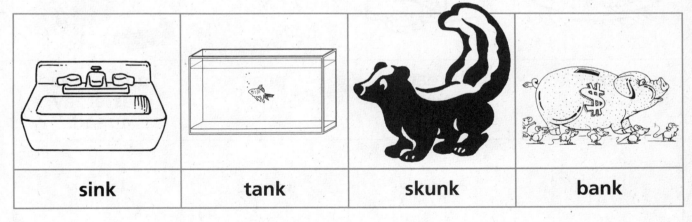

sink   tank   skunk   bank

PAIR and SHARE: Spelling
When spelling one of these words, listen for the /k/ sound at the end of the word. If you hear it, the word ends in *k*, not *g*.

ELPS 2.B recognize elements of the English sound system in newly acquired vocabulary • 3.A practice producing sounds of newly acquired vocabulary • 3.E share information in cooperative learning interactions • 4.A.1 learn relationships between sounds and letters of the English language • 4.A.2 decode words using a combination of skills

205

Phonics and Spelling Handbook

Other Vowel Pairs

 A. Vowel Pair *ea*

PHONICS The vowel pair *ea* usually stands for the long *e* sound as in *eat, beads,* and *heap*. This vowel pair also stands for two other sounds.

Listen as your teacher reads the words below.

PAIR and SHARE Circle the vowel pair in each word. Then read each word with your partner.

PAIR and SHARE:
Reading
Words spelled with *ea* can be a challenge to read and spell. Ask your teacher for help or look up the word in the dictionary.

long *a*	short *e*	long *e*	short *e* long *e*
steak	bread	peak	Today, I read. Yesterday, I read.

long *e*	short *e*	long *e*	long *a*
heat	head	tea	break

© HMH Supplemental Publishers Inc.

ELPS 2.B recognize elements of the English sound system in newly acquired vocabulary • 3.A practice producing sounds of newly acquired vocabulary • 4.A.1 learn relationships between sounds and letters of the English language • 4.A.2 decode words using a combination of skills

B. Vowel pair *oo*

PHONICS The vowel pair *oo* stands for more than one sound. Listen as your teacher reads the words below.

PAIR and SHARE:
Reading
Underline the vowel pair.
Then read the word.
Listen to your partner read.
Circle hard words.

moon

spoon

hoot

hoop

book

hook

cook

He took a rook.

PAIR and SHARE: Spelling
Words with the vowel sound in *moon* can be spelled in other ways, as in *dune* and *due*. Look up words with this sound in the dictionary if you are unsure how to spell them.

ELPS 2.B recognize elements of the English sound system in newly acquired vocabulary • 3.A practice producing sounds of newly acquired vocabulary • 3.E share information in cooperative learning interactions • 4.A.1 learn relationships between sounds and letters of the English language • 4.A.2 decode words using a combination of skills

Phonics and Spelling Handbook

Other Vowel Pairs

 C. Vowel Pairs *ue* and *ew*

PHONICS Long *u* has two sounds: the sound we hear in *cube* and the sound we hear in *tube*. These long *u* sounds can also be spelled with the letters *ue* and *ew*. Listen as your teacher reads each word.

PAIR and SHARE:
Reading
Read each word.
Listen to your partner read.
Circle hard words.

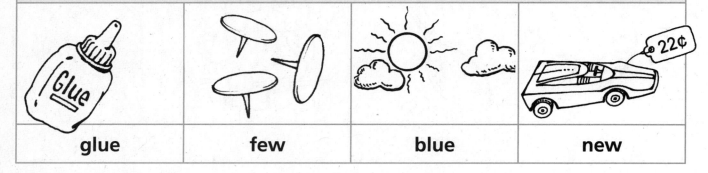

glue	few	blue	new

D. The Squawk Vowel

PHONICS That sounds like an odd name for a vowel! And this vowel is a bit odd! This sound can be spelled in a lot of ways. In fact, people often pronounce the word dog with this vowel sound.

alk	alt, aul, ault	all, oll	augh, ough	aw
balk	halt	ball	caught	paw
chalk	malt	call	taught	jaw
talk	salt	fall	bought	law
walk	Paul	mall	sought	raw
	Saul	doll	cough	saw
	fault			
	vault			

PAIR and SHARE: Spelling
Spelling words with vowel pairs can be challenging. Most sounds written with vowel pairs can be spelled in more than one way. Look up the spelling of words with these sounds if you are uncertain.

ELPS 2.B recognize elements of the English sound system in newly acquired vocabulary • 3.A practice producing sounds of newly acquired vocabulary • 3.E share information in cooperative learning interactions • 4.A.1 learn relationships between sounds and letters of the English language • 4.A.2 decode words using a combination of skills

Diphthongs

A. Sometimes, a vowel pair stands for two vowel sounds that glide into each other. This kind of vowel pair is called a *diphthong*.

PAIR and SHARE:
Reading

Listen as your teacher reads each word.
Circle the vowel pair.
Read the word. Listen to your partner read.

B. *oi* and *oy*

PHONICS These letters stand for the same diphthong. Listen as your teacher reads these words.

SPELLING NOTE:
At the end of a word, this diphthong is spelled *oy*. At the beginning or middle of a word, it is spelled *oi*.

| oink | toy | soil | coin |

C. *ou*

The letters *ou* can stand for the vowel sounds in *you*, *youth*, and *your*. These letters often stand for a diphthong, as in the words below.

SPELLING NOTE:
The *ou* diphthong can also be spelled with the letters *ow*, as in *cow*. Look up words with this sound if you are unsure of the spelling.

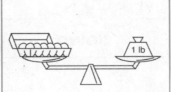

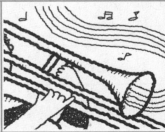

| hound | pound | ground | sound |

ELPS 2.B recognize elements of the English sound system in newly acquired vocabulary • 3.A practice producing sounds of newly acquired vocabulary • 3.E share information in cooperative learning interactions • 4.A.1 learn relationships between sounds and letters of the English language • 4.A.2 decode words using a combination of skills

209

Phonics and Spelling Handbook

Diphthongs

PAIR and SHARE:
Reading

Listen as your teacher reads each word.

Practice reading these words with your partner.

Look up the pronunciation of a word if you are not sure of the spelling.

 D. *ow*

PHONICS When the letter *w* is at the end of a word or syllable, it acts like a vowel. The letters *ow* are a vowel pair.

- These letters stand for the long vowel sound we hear in *crow*.

- They also stand for the diphthong we hear in *cow*.

There are no rules to use for pronouncing words spelled with *ow*.

crow	snow	cow	crown
bowl	mow	clown	howl

PAIR and SHARE: Spelling

The diphthong *ow* in *cow* is sometimes spelled in other words with *ou* (as in *round*). If you don't know how to spell a word with this sound, look it up.

ELPS 2.B recognize elements of the English sound system in newly acquired vocabulary • 3.A practice producing sounds of newly acquired vocabulary • 3.E share information in cooperative learning interactions • 4.A.1 learn relationships between sounds and letters of the English language • 4.A.2 decode words using a combination of skills

Vowels + r

PAIR and SHARE:
Reading
Listen as your teacher reads each word.
Repeat the word.
Listen to your partner read.

A. Vowels + r

PHONICS When the letter *r* follows a vowel, it can change the usual sound of the vowel.

B. *a + r*

PHONICS When followed by *r*, or *r* + a consonant, the letter *a* has the same sound that it does in words such as *pa, ma*, and *watch*. Read these words.

car	**star**	**yarn**

C. *or, oar, ore*

PHONICS In words spelled *or, oar*, and *ore*, the letter *r* changes the vowel sound. Read each word.

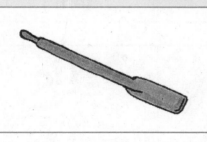		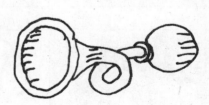
oar	**core**	**horn**

ELPS 2.B recognize elements of the English sound system in newly acquired vocabulary • 3.A practice producing sounds of newly acquired vocabulary • 3.E share information in cooperative learning interactions • 4.A.1 learn relationships between sounds and letters of the English language • 4.A.2 decode words using a combination of skills

211

Phonics and Spelling Handbook

 C. Exceptions

PHONICS In these words, you can hear the long vowel sound even though the letter *r* follows it.

steer	**pair**	**fire**

PAIR and SHARE:
Reading

Listen as your teacher reads each word.

Practice reading these words with your partner.

Note: some other words with these spellings may be pronounced differently. For example, *word* is not pronounced like *ford*.

Check the pronunciation of words with the letter patterns in a dictionary.

 D. Vowels Combined with *r*

PHONICS AND SPELLING In these words, the vowel combines with the *r*. Listen as your teacher reads each word. The vowel + *r* stands for the same in all of these words, but the vowel letter can be *e, i, o,* or *u*. That makes spelling difficult!

bird	**fir**	**fur**	**fern**

herd	**shirt**	**skirt**	**words**

PAIR and SHARE: Spelling
Words with one of the vowel letters i, u, e, or o that is followed by the letter r may all sound alike. Look up the spelling of these words in a dictionary if you are not sure which vowel letter to use.

Silent Letters

Silent Letters	Example Words				
b	numb	comb	lamb	climb	crumb
g	sign				
gh	eight	thought	straight	height	light	right
k	know	knew	knit	knock	knee	knife
l	calf	half	talk	walk	would	should
t	castle	fasten	whistle			
w	wrap	write	wrote	written	wreck	wrong

ELPS 2.B recognize elements of the English sound system in newly acquired vocabulary • 3.A practice producing sounds of newly acquired vocabulary • 4.A.1 learn relationships between sounds and letters of the English language • 4.A.2 decode words using a combination of skills

213

Phonics and Spelling Handbook

PHONOLOGY: CONSONANT BLENDS WITH /S/

A.   Initial Blends with s

When a word begins with *s* + one or more consonant letters, be sure to pronounce all consonant sounds.

Practice with these words. Make a difference in how the words in each group sound.

sip, slip, skip	soup, stoop, sloop	sell, smell, spell
side, slide, snide	Sam, slam, scam	seep, steep, sleep
sub, snub, stub	sat, scat, slat	sop, stop, slop

B.   Final Blends with s

When a word ends with *s* + one or more consonant letters, make sure you pronounce all of the consonant sounds. Say each consonant sound in the order it occurs in the word.

Practice with these words. Make a difference in how the words in each group sound.

lass, last, lasts	Tess, test, tests	less, lest, let's
mass, mast, masts	miss, mist, mists	Wes, west, wets
lap, laps, lapse	loss, lost, lots	Gus, gust, gusts

© HMH Supplemental Publishers Inc.

ELPS 2.B recognize elements of the English sound system in newly acquired vocabulary • 2.E.3 use linguistic support to confirm understanding • 3.A practice producing sounds of newly acquired vocabulary

PHONOLOGY: CONSONANT BLENDS WITH /S/

C. Ask

When you say the word *ask,* pronounce it so that it sounds different from the word *ax.* The word *ask* rhymes with *task, mask,* and *bask.*

D. Word Sort

Which words have /sk/ sounds? Which words have /ks/ sounds? Write words in the first row that end in /sk/ sounds.

Write words in the second row that end in /ks/ sounds.

task	mask	tax
max	backs	ask
desk	oaks	risk

Row 1: /sk/ _____

Row 2: /ks/ _____

Practice reading these sentences. Pay close attention to how you pronounce the colored letters.

1. I have pins and ta**ck**s.

2. Did you wear that ma**sk**?

3. Did you a**sk** me a question?

4. Can you move those de**sk**s?

5. He a**sk**ed me politely!

ELPs 2.B recognize elements of the English sound system in newly acquired vocabulary • 2.E.3 use linguistic support to confirm understanding • 3.A practice producing sounds of newly acquired vocabulary

215

Phonics and Spelling Handbook

PHONOLOGY: CONSONANT BLENDS WITH /S/

> **E. Other Initial Blends**
>
> Some words begin with three consonants, as in *strong*. Some begin with one single consonant and a consonant digraph, as in *shrink*. Be sure to pronounce all consonants sounds in the order they occur in the word.

Practice with these words.

stream, scream	strap, scrap	stroll, scroll
shrimp, scrimp,	shrub, scrub	shriek, screech

> **F. Other Final Blends**
>
> Make sure you pronounce all of the consonant sounds in a word. Say each consonant sound in the order it occurs.

Practice with these words. Make a difference in how the words in each group sound.

1.	rap, raps, rapt	pack, pact, packs	men, mend, mends
2.	an, and, hands	fine, find, finds	give, gift, gifts
3.	chip, chimp, chimps	pick, pink, ping	kick, kink, king
4.	putt, punt, punts	set, sent, sends	truck, trunk, trunks
5.	lit, lift, lifts	correct, corrected	land, lands, landing

ELPs 2.B recognize elements of the English sound system in newly acquired vocabulary • 2.E.3 use linguistic support to confirm understanding • 3.A practice producing sounds of newly acquired vocabulary

Check Your Progress

LEARNING STRATEGIES

You are learning English in so many ways! Check the boxes to show how much progress you've made. Check all boxes that apply.

- ☐ I pronounce English words better than I did before.
- ☐ I can spell correctly.
- ☐ I use new words when I speak.
- ☐ I use new words in my writing.
- ☐ I use pictures, charts, graphs, and maps to help me understand words.
- ☐ When I see or hear an unfamiliar word or expression, I'm better at figuring out its meaning.
- ☐ I know much more about English grammar.
- ☐ I know how to speak to teachers and adults, and how to speak to my friends.
- ☐ I ask for help when I don't understand.
- ☐ I've gotten better at recognizing and correcting mistakes in my writing.

I'M LISTENING!

Check the boxes to show the ways you have become a better listener.
Check all boxes that apply.

- ☐ I know which letters stand for sounds in words that I hear.

- ☐ I watch people's gestures and expressions to help me understand spoken English.

- ☐ I understand more of what I see and hear in newspapers and magazines, and on television, radio, and the Internet.

- ☐ I understand more of what people say about topics I already know.

- ☐ I understand more of what people say about topics I don't already know.

- ☐ I take notes to help me understand spoken English.

- ☐ I'm better at answering questions about stories and information that I hear.

- ☐ I understand more of my teacher's directions, and I can repeat them.

- ☐ When people speak, I understand faster and better than I did before.

SAY IT ALOUD

Check the boxes to show the ways you have become a better speaker. Check all boxes that apply.

☐ I know how to pronounce words better than I did before.

☐ I can describe people, places, and things better than I could before.

☐ I can use both simple and complex sentences when I speak.

☐ I use vocabulary words correctly when I speak.

☐ I can share information with my classmates when we work together.

☐ I know how to ask for help when I need it.

☐ I'm better at expressing ideas, opinions, and feelings.

☐ I can tell about events better than I could before.

☐ I'm better at retelling stories that I have read.

☐ I know how to speak to teachers and adults and how to speak to my friends.

READ IT!

Check the boxes to show the ways you have become a better reader.
Check all boxes that apply.

☐ I know how to read more words, including longer words.

☐ I recognize more high-frequency words than I did before.

☐ I understand more of the words that I see around me at school, at home, and in my town.

☐ I use pictures to help me understand what I read.

☐ I can use what I already know to understand new topics.

☐ I can use information from classroom discussions to help me understand reading selections.

☐ If I don't know a word, I can figure out the meaning by looking at nearby words and sentences.

☐ I can talk about and retell reading selections better than I could before.

☐ I ask for help from my classmates and teacher when I don't understand.

☐ I can take notes about reading selections.

☐ I can answer questions about reading selections.

☐ I read better, faster, and with greater understanding than I did before.

Check Your Progress

WRITE IT!

Check the boxes to show the ways you have become a better writer.
Check all boxes that apply.

☐ I'm better at spelling high-frequency words than I was before.

☐ I use high-frequency words correctly in my writing.

☐ I'm better at using spelling rules to write new words.

☐ I use vocabulary words correctly in my writing.

☐ I use a variety of sentence types and lengths when I write.

☐ I'm better at applying grammar rules in my writing.

☐ I can edit my writing to correct mistakes and make it better.

☐ I can describe events in writing better than I could before.

☐ I'm better at giving information in writing.

☐ I'm better at expressing ideas in writing.

☐ I can write better and faster than I could before.

Index for Handbooks

Standardized Test Practice

Standardized Test-Taking Tips

Cut out the tips below and use them with the Standardized Test Practice.

Practice Test 1

Read this selection. Then read each question and fill in the correct answer.

The Pine Needle

September Issue
Page 3

Serving the Students of
Lakeville Grade School

Getting Checked Out
by Diane Jones

1   Do you know why it is important to have a yearly health checkup? To find out, I interviewed Doctor Louise Winston. Her answers to my questions helped me understand why a checkup is important. Then she gave me a checkup.

2   "A yearly checkup helps me to know that all systems are go with each patient," Doctor Winston explained. "The checkup starts when my patient steps on the scale. Each patient should be weighed and measured at least once a year. That way, I keep track of how much my patient has grown."

3   Doctor Winston showed me a blood pressure machine. It has a cuff that goes around your arm. She wrapped the cuff around my arm. She squeezed a bulb at the end of the cuff to make it inflate. The cuff filled with air. It got tighter and tighter on my arm. This helped the doctor tell how well blood was sent to my heart. "Your blood pressure is fine," Doctor Winston said with a smile.

4   Next, she shined a light in my eyes. The tool she used looked like a small flashlight. "I use this to check your eyes," she said. After, I read an eye chart. The letters at the top were very big, but the lower letters got smaller and smaller. I read most of the letters, and Doctor Winston said that my eyesight was great.

5   After checking my eyes, she hit my knee with a tool that looked like a little rubber hammer. My leg jumped up!

6   "Good," Doctor Winston said. "That means your brain sent a message telling your leg to move."

Continued on next page

GO ON

Getting Checked Out *continued*

7   Doctor Winston took out a wooden stick. She put the stick on my tongue.

8   "I'm holding your tongue down to make room to get a good look inside your throat," she said. "I can see that your tonsils look nice and healthy."

9   My favorite part of my checkup was when Doctor Winston let me use a special tool to listen to my heart. A stethoscope has earplugs attached to a long tube with a round part at the bottom. She put the earplugs in my ears and the round part on my chest. I heard a *boom da boom da boom.*

10   Then Doctor Winston listened. "Your heart is working just fine," she said. "Now, take a deep breath so I can listen to your lungs."

11   I took a big breath. "Your lungs sound really good," Doctor Winston said with a grin.

12   Finally, Doctor Winston asked me to stand up, bend over, and touch my toes. "I'm doing this to check your back and make sure that everything is straight and strong," she explained.

13   "You're in great shape," Doctor Winston said. "Your checkup is over. See you next year!"

14   It's good to know that everything is fine, but sometimes there is something that's not quite right. A yearly checkup can help the doctor find out if something needs more care. There's no easier way to stay healthy than by getting checked out every year.

1   In paragraph 1, which words help the reader know what <u>interviewed</u> means?

   ⬭ *helped me understand*
   ⬭ *Her answers to my questions*
   ⬭ *she gave me a checkup*
   ⬭ *a checkup is important*

   TEKS 3.4B

2   Paragraph 3 is mostly about —

   ⬭ how a stethoscope works
   ⬭ the parts of a blood pressure cuff
   ⬭ how a blood pressure machine works
   ⬭ why it is important to have good blood pressure

   TEKS RC-3(D)

GO ON ➡

3 What is the title of this article?

◯ *The Pine Needle*

◯ *Keeping Healthy*

◯ *Getting Checked Out*

◯ *Diane Jones*

TEKS 3.15B

4 Which sentence from the story shows the reader why getting a yearly checkup is important?

◯ *Her answers to my questions helped me understand why a checkup is important.*

◯ *Each patient should be weighed and measured at least once a year.*

◯ *A yearly checkup can help the doctor find out if something needs more care.*

◯ *My favorite part of my checkup was when Doctor Winston let me use a special tool to listen to my heart.*

TEKS 3.13A

5 Why does Doctor Winston hit her patient's knee with a rubber hammer?

◯ To check that the body receives messages from the brain

◯ To find out if it hurts

◯ To see if the patient's leg is strong

◯ To be sure that the patient can feel the hammer

TEKS RC-3(D)

6 Use the chart below to answer the question.

What Happens	Why It Happens
The doctor uses a stick to hold the tongue down.	???

Which of the following belongs in the empty box?

◯ To check the lungs

◯ To make room to see inside the throat

◯ To see the back teeth

◯ To check that the patient can say "AHH" with the stick in her mouth

TEKS 3.13C

7 In paragraph 3, what does <u>inflate</u> mean?

◯ Become tight

◯ Fill with air

◯ Cause pressure

◯ Make blood flow

TEKS 3.4B

8 Which word from paragraph 1 means about the same as the word <u>understand</u>?

◯ *important*

◯ *questions*

◯ *checkup*

◯ *know*

TEKS 3.4C

GO ON

> **Read this selection. Then read each question and fill in the correct answer.**

Spaghetti Sauce for Tommy

1   Tommy was shooting hoops in the backyard when he smelled Mom's special spaghetti sauce in the air. He put away his basketball and headed straight to the kitchen.

2   Mom was stirring a pot of red sauce with a wooden spoon. She dipped a piece of bread into the sauce and tasted it. Then she added other <u>ingredients</u> such as chopped peppers, garlic, and onion.

3   Mom dipped some bread in the sauce for Tommy. "Yum," he said. "Who taught you how to make such good sauce?"

4   "Grandma Angelina," Mom said. "When I was your age, I helped her in the kitchen."

5   "You know," Mom went on, "your Grandma came to America from a small Italian village. She and Grandpa had a farm near Granger, Texas. They worked very hard. They grew lots of vegetables, and their tomatoes were the best in the county."

6   "Grandma made spaghetti sauce from those tomatoes," Mom went on. "First, she'd drop tomatoes in a pot of boiling water for about a minute. Then she'd put them a bowl of ice water."

7   "Why did she make the tomatoes hot and then make them cold?" Tommy asked.

8   "So the tomato skin would slip off very easily," Mom answered. "You wouldn't like tomato skin in spaghetti sauce, would you?" Tommy shook his head. He couldn't talk because his mouth was full of bread!

9   "Grandma put the tomatoes in a large pot," Mom continued. "She'd <u>simmer</u> them on a low flame so that they'd cook very slowly. Then she'd add garlic, onion, spices, and sometimes a little bit of sugar."

© HMH Supplemental Publishers Inc.

GO ON ▶

10   "I stirred the sauce and listened to Grandma tell about her village in Italy," Mom continued.

11   "What stories did she tell you?" Tommy asked.

12   "Well, Grandma's village was high up on a mountain," Mom began. "School was in a town at the bottom of the mountain. Every day Grandma's father, your great-grandfather, took the village children down the mountain to school."

13   "Grandma said there was this pesky boy named Tonio who pulled her pigtails in school. She got so mad that she asked her father not to let him in the cart the next day."

14   "Then how did Tonio get to school?" Tommy asked.

15   "Well, he woke up very early the next morning," Mom said. "He walked all the way down the mountain to the school. He didn't pull Grandma's pigtails that day. He was asleep at his desk!"

16   "How did he get home?" Tommy asked.

17   "Grandma took pity on Tonio and asked her father to let him ride back in the cart."

18   "Grandma and Tony became good friends. When they grew up, they got married! That boy was your Grandpa Tony!"

19   "Then one day, your great-grandfather took Grandma and Grandpa down the mountain in the mule cart for the last time," Mom said. "He took them to the boat that brought them to America."

20   "Grandma said that her father handed her a note just before she got on the boat," Mom told Tommy. "It was a recipe for spaghetti sauce! And it was called *Tomasina's Sauce*."

21   "Who was Tomasina?" Tommy asked.

© HMH Supplemental Publishers Inc.

GO ON

22 Mom squeezed Tommy and said, "Tomasina was your great-grandmother."

23 Tommy licked the spoon. "This sauce is just right," he said.

24 "That's because you are a great stirrer," Mom said. "We'll just call this *Tommy's Sauce!*".

25 "What would Grandma Angelina think about that?" asked Tommy.

26 Mom smiled, "She would say *molto bono*, which means 'very good' in Italian."

27 "Let's tell Grandma about *Tommy's Sauce*," Tommy said. "We can tell her that it's *molto bono*!"

28 Mom laughed and gave Tommy a great big hug. "You're *molto bono*," she said.

9 What does the word <u>simmer</u> mean in paragraph 9?

◯ Put in a large pot
◯ Cook slowly
◯ Add garlic
◯ Peel tomatoes

TEKS 3.4B

10 Tommy goes to his mom's kitchen because —

◯ his mother asked him to stir the sauce
◯ he wants to find out who taught Mom how to make the sauce
◯ he wants to learn about his Grandma's village
◯ he smells his mother's sauce cooking

TEKS RC-3(D)

GO ON ➤

11 Paragraph 12 is mostly about —

⬭ Grandma's village

⬭ Grandma's school

⬭ how village children got to school

⬭ Tommy's great-grandfather

TEKS RC-3(D)

12 What causes Mom to tell Tommy a story about Grandma's village?

⬭ Cooking with Tommy reminds Mom of the stories Grandma told as she cooked.

⬭ Tommy is curious about Grandma's village.

⬭ Mom wants Tommy to know how hard it was for Grandma to get to school.

⬭ Mom wants Tommy to know about his great-grandfather.

TEKS RC-3(D)

13 Which is the best summary of this story?

⬭ Tommy plays basketball and stirs spaghetti sauce.

⬭ Mom tells Tommy a story about how his grandparents first met.

⬭ Tommy helps his mother make sauce and learns about his family.

⬭ Tommy learns that the words *molto bono* mean "very good."

TEKS 3.8A

14 Which of these best describes how Tommy feels about his mother's sauce?

⬭ He thinks it is delicious.

⬭ He does not like it.

⬭ He doesn't want any.

⬭ He thinks it is too spicy.

TEKS 3.8B

15 In paragraph 2, which words help the reader know what ingredients means?

⬭ *Peppers, garlic, and onions*

⬭ *Dipped a piece of bread*

⬭ *Tasted the bread*

⬭ *A wooden spoon*

TEKS 3.4B

16 Look at the chart below.

Making Spaghetti Sauce

Drop tomatoes in boiling water

↓

↓

Remove tomato skin

↓

Simmer tomatoes in a pot

Which belongs in the empty box?

⬭ Add garlic

⬭ Put tomatoes in ice water

⬭ Stir the sauce

⬭ Put tomatoes in a large pot

TEKS 3.8A

GO ON

> **Read this selection. Then read each question and fill in the correct answer.**

Frogs and Toads

1   "I have a surprise," Mr. Waters said to his third-grade class. "We're going to take a class trip to the Parkland Zoo."

2   The class started chattering noisily, asking one question after another. "When are we going?" "How long will we be there?" "Will we get lunch at the zoo?"

3   "Calm down, class," Mr. Waters laughed. "All the information about the trip is on a form for your parents. It also tells them that we've been learning about animals that can live in or out of the water. That explains why we'll be going to the <u>amphibian</u> house at the zoo. So, what kinds of animals are amphibians?"

4   "Salamanders are amphibians," Marcy answered.

5   "That's right," Mr. Waters said. "Who can name two more?"

6   "I can," Shawn said. "Frogs and toads are both amphibians."

7   "That's only one animal," Rosa said. "Toads are the same as frogs."

8   "No, they're not," Shawn said. Rosa disagreed, though.

9   Shawn and Rosa argued until Mr. Waters <u>interrupted</u> them to say, "You're both right. Toads *are* in the frog family, but they are not exactly the same as frogs."

10   "They both lay eggs in the water to hatch their baby tadpoles, though," Josh said. "That's the same for frogs and toads."

11   "That's right, Josh," Mr. Waters said. "Though frogs lay eggs in clusters, or lumps. Toads lay eggs in long lines like chains."

GO ON

12   "Both frog and toad tadpoles breathe with gills," Maria added. "When they grow up, the tadpoles develop lungs to breathe air."

13   "I can tell you something different about frogs and toads," Ricardo said. "Someone told me that you can get warts from touching a toad."

14   "Some people think that, but it's not true. Toads have dry, warty skin, but you can't get warts from them." Mr. Waters continued, "Ricardo, how is a frog's skin different from a toad's skin?"

15   "Well," Ricardo began. "A frog's skin is smooth and slimy. I guess that's one difference between a frog and a toad."

16   "Here's another," Mr. Waters went on. "A frog has long legs so it can jump. Toads have short legs. They can only hop."

17   Lu Ann raised her hand. "My dad is reading me a story about a jumping frog contest," she said. "I guess there aren't any stories about jumping toad contests!" Lu Ann said.

18   "Now, here's one more difference that will surprise you," Mr. Waters said. "Frogs have teeth and toads don't."

19   "Yikes," Shawn and Rosa said at the same time. "You mean a frog could bite us?"

20   "I don't think so. They only have teeth in the top of their jaws," Mr. Waters said. "They also have long sticky tongues," he added. "They catch insects that way. Toads have sticky tongues, too."

21   "Here's another difference," Lu Ann said. "If you kiss a frog, it may turn into a prince! But who wants to kiss a frog?"

22   Everyone laughed, including Mr. Waters. "Now, let's get serious for a minute," he said. "I want you to think about what we learned today. Then, when we go to the amphibian house, you can pick out the frogs from the toads."

© HMH Supplemental Publishers Inc.

GO ON

17 The students in Mr. Waters's class will go to the zoo to —

- ⬭ get lunch at the zoo
- ⬭ see salamanders
- ⬭ watch tadpoles grow
- ⬭ visit the amphibian house

TEKS RC-3(D)

18 What is the main problem in the story?

- ⬭ Rosa and Shawn have an argument.
- ⬭ The students have to tell why they are going to visit the amphibian house.
- ⬭ The students have to learn the difference between a frog and a toad.
- ⬭ Touching toads causes warts.

TEKS RC-3(D)

19 Read the meanings below for the word raise.

> **raise** ('r ā z) *verb*
> **1.** to lift, to move higher
> **2.** to help grow
> **3.** to take care of
> **4.** to collect, to earn

Which meaning best fits the way raised is used in paragraph 17?

- ⬭ Meaning 1
- ⬭ Meaning 2
- ⬭ Meaning 3
- ⬭ Meaning 4

TEKS 3.4B

20 In paragraph 3, what does amphibian mean?

- ⬭ A form for parents
- ⬭ A house at the zoo
- ⬭ An animal that can live in or out of water
- ⬭ Information about the trip to the zoo

TEKS 3.4B

21 This story was written mainly to —

- ⬭ explain how frogs and toads are alike and different
- ⬭ show that Mr. Waters is a good teacher
- ⬭ explain how frogs and toads lay their eggs
- ⬭ explain what an amphibian is

TEKS 3.12

22 How do tadpoles breathe before they grow lungs?

- ⬭ Only on the land
- ⬭ With special tanks
- ⬭ With gills
- ⬭ With long legs

TEKS 3.8A

GO ON ▶

23   Look as the diagram about frogs and toads. Answer the question that follows.

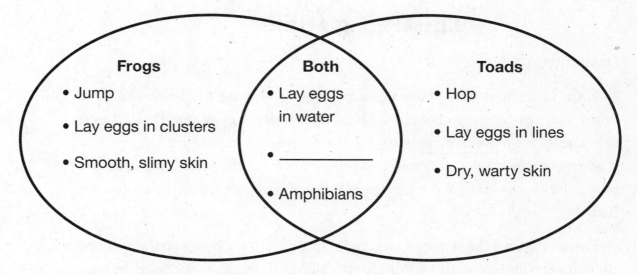

Frogs
- Jump
- Lay eggs in clusters
- Smooth, slimy skin

Both
- Lay eggs in water
- _____
- Amphibians

Toads
- Hop
- Lay eggs in lines
- Dry, warty skin

Which of the following goes in the blank?

    Have short legs
    Have teeth
    Are in the frog family
    Have long legs

TEKS 3.15B

24   Which of these **BEST** describes how the students feel about going to the zoo?

    Amused
    Afraid
    Excited
    Bored

TEKS 3.8B

25   What subject would you say that Mr. Waters class is studying in this selection?

    Math
    Science
    Reading
    Social Studies

TEKS 3.13B

26   In paragraph 9, the word <u>interrupted</u> means —

    argued
    stopped
    laughed
    yelled

TEKS 3.4B

GO ON

Read the two selections that follow.

The Garage Sale

Dear Judy,

1   I am so excited that you will be coming to visit us in two weeks. Dad and I can really use your help with our plans for a garage sale. Dad says the garage is so <u>overflowing</u> with stuff that we can hardly get the car into it anymore. He thinks we should sell the stuff we don't need. You and I can set up our own section of the garage sale. Maybe we can call it "Stuff Just for Kids."

2   For example, I have some electronic games that I never use anymore. Remember the one with the different colored lights that we used to play together years ago? You know, the lights would come on in a different <u>sequence</u> each time. Then we would have to push the colors to repeat in the same order. I'm going to sell it, unless you want it. I am also going to sell my old roller skates. Dad gave me a set of in-line skates last year!

3   Mom and Dad are going through their stuff, too. You wouldn't believe the junk they have. They even have records! I told them that no one uses records anymore. "Most everyone listens to CDs or MP3 players," I told them. They think that some people would love to have their old records. We'll see at the garage sale.

4   Do you have stuff to sell at our "Stuff Just for Kids" table? Bring it with you when your Mom drives you down. I bet you will be happy to get rid of things you don't use anymore.

5   We'll have to spend a day putting price tags on our stuff and helping Dad make signs telling about our sale. We'll also help him put up the signs around the neighborhood. Then we'll set up and spend the next day selling. It should be a lot of fun. We'll make some money, too!

Love,
Jill

GO ON

Kidding Around

A Magazine for 7- to 10-Year-Olds

September, 2009   Vol. 5. Issue 3

Money-Making Ideas for Kids

by Gia Treadwell

1   Is there a toy or game you'd like to buy? Perhaps you'd like to give a gift to a friend. Either way, you probably need to earn some money. Fortunately, there are lots of ways kids can earn money.

2   You can earn money right around your own house. Make a list of chores that you'd help out with and tell what you'd charge. For example, you can match socks on laundry day and charge a nickel a pair. Of course, you can't charge for chores you're already expected to do.

3   Assisting a neighbor is a good way to make extra money. First, make sure that your parents know the neighbor well and agree to your plan. If your neighbor has a pet, you can pet sit. That means you'll feed the pet and make sure it's okay while the neighbor is away. Don't take a job if you have to walk the pet though. Wait until you're older to do that.

4   When a neighbor goes away, you can also tend the garden. All you have to do is water the plants. If you live in an apartment building, you can pick up mail or newspapers. Put up a sign on your door to let neighbors know that you're available to do these jobs!

5   It just takes one good idea to get started making some extra nickels, dimes, and even dollars! Don't get carried away, though. Remember, you have to make time to do your homework, do your regular chores, play with your friends, and just relax.

GO ON

Use "The Garage Sale" (p. 115) to answer questions 27–31.

27 What is the main problem in this story?

◯ There's too much stuff in Jill's garage.

◯ Jill has too many stuffed animals.

◯ Jill's dad does not want to sell anything.

◯ No one listens to records anymore.

TEKS RC-3(D)

28 In paragraph 1, which words help the reader know what <u>overflowing</u> means?

◯ *use your help*

◯ *sell the stuff we don't need*

◯ *can hardly get the car into it*

◯ *coming to visit*

TEKS 3.4B

29 How can you tell that Jill and Judy have been friends for a long time?

◯ They played together with an electric game a long time ago.

◯ Jill's parents have records.

◯ Judy is coming to visit Jill.

◯ Jill and Judy will work together to make a "Stuff for Kids" table.

TEKS 3.13B

30 In paragraph 2, the word <u>sequence</u> means —

◯ repeat in the same order

◯ different colored lights

◯ push the colors

◯ the lights would come on

TEKS 3.4B

31 Use the chart below to answer the question.

What Happens	Why It Happens
Jill is going to sell her old roller skates.	???

Which of the following belongs in the empty box?

◯ She got in-line skates last year.

◯ Jill and Judy have the same shoe size.

◯ Judy is going to try on Jill's skates.

◯ No one will buy old records.

TEKS 3.13C

© HMH Supplemental Publishers Inc.

GO ON

> **Use "Money-Making Ideas for Kids" (p. 116) to answer questions 32–34.**

32 The author of this selection is trying to —

- ⬭ persuade the reader to think about saving money
- ⬭ inform the reader about ways to earn some extra money
- ⬭ entertain the reader with a story about pet-sitting
- ⬭ persuade the reader to water a neighbor's plants

TEKS 3.12

33 In paragraph 3, the word <u>assisting</u> means —

- ⬭ avoiding
- ⬭ helping
- ⬭ calling
- ⬭ finding

TEKS 3.4B

34 What is the title of this article?

- ⬭ *Kidding Around Reporter*
- ⬭ *A Magazine for 7- to 10-Year-Olds*
- ⬭ *Gia Treadwell*
- ⬭ *Money-Making Ideas for Kids*

TEKS 3.15B

GO ON

Use "The Garage Sale" and "Money-Making Ideas for Kids" to answer questions 35–36.

---

35 These selections are both mostly about —

◯ ways kids can earn extra money

◯ ways kids can help their neighbors

◯ ways kids can repair broken toys

◯ ways kids can work together to sort their toys

TEKS RC-3(D)

36 "Money-Making Ideas for Kids" is different from "The Garage Sale" because the article —

◯ tells how to decide what to sell and what to keep

◯ tells how to organize a garage sale

◯ suggests many different ways to earn extra money

◯ tells how a garage sale can help kids earn extra money

TEKS RC-3(D)

STOP

Practice Test 2

Read the writing prompt. Use your own paper to respond to the prompt.

Write a composition about an animal that you would like to have as a pet.

The information below will remind you what to think about as you write.

REMEMBER—YOU SHOULD

❏ follow the steps to plan, draft, revise, and edit your writing

❏ write about an animal that you would like to have as a pet

❏ write a main idea sentence that names the animal and tells why you like it

❏ write detail sentences that tell about the animal so that the reader really understands why you chose that animal

❏ try to use correct spelling, capitalization, punctuation, grammar, and sentences

GO ON

> **Read the introduction and the passage that follows. Then read each question and fill in the correct answer.**

Mai read about Grandma Moses, a famous folk artist. Mai decided to write a report about her. Read the report. Think of how to make Mai's sentences better. Then answer the questions.

Grandma Moses

(1) Anna Robertson is beter known as the folk artist Grandma Moses. (2) Folk artists are artists who dont have any training.

(3) She was a painter. (4) She began painting as a hobby when she was about 75. (5) Her paintings tell stories of her simple life in hoosick falls, a small town in upstate New York. (6) She painted pictures of sleigh rides in the snow, farmhouses, and country holidays. (7) Her paintings were shown at county fairs and hung in store windows.

(8) An art collector named Louis Caldor visited Hoosick Falls on a trip through upstate New York. (9) He liked the paintings that he saw in a store window. (10) The storeowner told Caldor that the artist lived in a farm up the road. (11) Caldor went their and met Grandma Moses. (12) He liked the farm.

(13) Grandma Moses showed Caldor more paintings. (14) Grandma Moses became one of the most famous folk artists in America. (15) She is still famous today, although she died in 1961 at the age of 101.

---

1 What change, if any, should be made in sentence 1?

- ⬭ Change *folk artist* to **Folk Artist**
- ⬭ Change *known* to **know**
- ⬭ Change *beter* to **better**
- ⬭ Make no change

TEKS 3.24B

2 What change, if any, should be made in sentence 2?

- ⬭ Change *dont* to **do'nt**
- ⬭ Change *dont* to **don't**
- ⬭ Change *dont* to **do'not**
- ⬭ Make no change

TEKS 3.23C

GO ON ➡

3 What is the **BEST** way to combine sentences 3 and 4?

⬭ At 75, Grandma Moses began painting as a hobby.

⬭ She began painting at 75.

⬭ She began painting. She was 75.

⬭ She was 75, so she began painting.

TEKS 3.22B

4 What change, if any, should be made to sentence 5?

⬭ Change *hoosick falls* to **Hoosick falls**

⬭ Change *hoosick falls* to **hoosick Falls**

⬭ Change *hoosick falls* to **Hoosick Falls**

⬭ Make no change

TEKS 3.23B

5 What change, if any, should be made to sentence 11?

⬭ Change *their* to **there**

⬭ Change *met* to **meet**

⬭ Insert a comma before *and*

⬭ Make no change

TEKS 3.24E

6 Which sentence does **NOT** belong in this report?

⬭ Sentence 4

⬭ Sentence 8

⬭ Sentence 10

⬭ Sentence 12

TEKS 3.17D

7 Which sentence could **BEST** be added after sentence 13?

⬭ There were a lot of paintings to show.

⬭ He took them to his art gallery, and they were bought by museums.

⬭ No one wanted to buy the paintings.

⬭ Grandma Moses didn't like the gallery.

TEKS 3.17C

GO ON

> **Read the introduction and the passage that follows. Then read each question and fill in the correct answer.**

Jack wrote about his cat, Puff. He wants you to read his paper and help him improve it. As you read, think about suggestions you would give Jack. Then answer the questions.

My Cat Puff

(1) When Puff was a kitten, it looked like a puffball. (2) Thats how Puff got his name. (3) My brother said cats are too hard to care for. (4) My brother is wrong.

(5) I think cats are easyer to care for than dogs. (6) Cats don't need to be walked. (7) They indoor pets. (8) Cats need some care, though. (9) Their kitty litter needs to be kept clean. (10) I don't mind. (11) Their coats need brushing. (12) Their nails need cutting. (13) Puff loves when his coat is brushed, but not when his nails are cut.

(14) Some times Puff sleeps in my bed. (15) He cuddles up next to me and purrs in my ear loudly. (16) I don't mind, though, because his purring is like music to my ears. (17) Puff is the perfect pet or should I say "purrfect"?

---

8 What change, if any, should be made to sentence 1?

- ⬭ Change *it* to **its**
- ⬭ Change *Puff* to **puff**
- ⬭ Change *it* to **he**
- ⬭ Make no change

TEKS 3.17C

9 What change, if any, should be made to sentence 2?

- ⬭ Change *his* to **it's**
- ⬭ Change *Thats* to **That's**
- ⬭ Change *Puff* to **puff**
- ⬭ Make no change

TEKS 3.23C

GO ON ➡

10 What is the **BEST** way to combine sentences 3 and 4?

⬭ My brother said cats are hard to care for, so he's wrong.

⬭ My brother is wrong. Cats are hard to care for.

⬭ My brother said cats are too hard to care for, but he is wrong.

⬭ My brother said he is wrong.

TEKS 3.17C

11 What change, if any, should be made to sentence 5?

⬭ Change *easyer* to **easier**

⬭ Change *cats* to **cat**

⬭ Change *cats* to **cat's**

⬭ Make no change

TEKS 3.24B

12 Which sentence could **BEST** be added after sentence 9?

⬭ Bags of kitty litter are heavy.

⬭ Some kids hate cleaning litter.

⬭ The kitty litter box is plastic.

⬭ Kitty litter is like sand.

TEKS 3.17C

13 What is the **BEST** way to combine sentences 11 and 12?

⬭ Their coats need brushing and their nails need cutting.

⬭ Coats and nails need cutting.

⬭ Their coat needs brushing, because their nails need cutting.

⬭ Their coats need brushing although they need cutting.

TEKS 3.22A

14 Which of the following is not a complete sentence?

⬭ Sentence 4

⬭ Sentence 7

⬭ Sentence 13

⬭ Sentence 17

TEKS 3.22C

15 What change, if any, should be made to sentence 14?

⬭ Change *Puff* to **puff**

⬭ Change *sleeps* to **sleep**

⬭ Change *Some times* to **Sometimes**

⬭ Make no change.

TEKS 3.24D

16 What change, if any, should be made to sentence 15?

⬭ He cuddles up to me and purr in my ear loudly.

⬭ He cuddles up to me, and purrs in my ear loudly.

⬭ He cuddles up to me and purrs loudly in my ear.

⬭ Make no change

TEKS 3.22A

GO ON

> **Read the introduction and the passage that follows. Then read each question and fill in the correct answer.**

Judy wrote a report on American schoolhouses of 200 years ago. Read her report. Think about how to make her sentences better. Then answer the questions.

A One-Room Schoolhouse

(1) About 200 years ago, most children in America went to a schoolhouse that had only one room. (2) Children from the first to the eighth grades were taught they're lessons in that one classroom. (3) Sum one-room schools had as many as 40 children. (4) Others had as few as six. (5) One teacher taught reading writing math history English and all other subjects.

(6) The teacher's desk was at the front of the room facing them. (7) The youngest children sat. (8) In the front of the room. (9) They wore old-fashioned clothes. (10) The oldest children sat in the back. (11) In some schools, the boys sat on one side of the room. (12) The girls sat on the other side of the room. (13) When the teacher called on a student, they stood up and answered the question. (14) The children who were in the same grade listened to the teacher's lesson. (15) The other children sat quietly reading their books or sat quietly writing their lessons while other children were reading their books.

(16) Would you like to be in a one-room schoolhouse. (17) As to me, I just don't know what I'd want. (18) We get along now, but who knows how wed feel after years and years in the same room?

---

17 What change, if any, should be made in sentence 2?

 ◯ Change *classroom* to **class room**

 ◯ Change *they're* to **there**

 ◯ Change *they're* to **their**

 ◯ Make no change

TEKS 3.23C

18 What change, if any, should be made in sentence 3?

 ◯ Change *Sum* to **Some**

 ◯ Change *children* to **childs**

 ◯ Change *many* to **mini**

 ◯ Make no change

TEKS 3.24E

GO ON ➡

19 What is the **BEST** way to revise sentence 5?

⬭ That one teacher taught reading. That teacher taught writing and math. That teacher taught English and all other subjects.

⬭ That one teacher taught reading, writing, math, history, English, and all other subjects.

⬭ That one teacher taught. Writing and math. English and all other subjects.

⬭ That one teacher taught reading, writing, math, history. And English and all other subjects.

TEKS 3.23C

20 The meaning of sentence 6 can be improved by changing *them* to —

⬭ each classroom

⬭ herself

⬭ the children

⬭ school

TEKS 3.17C

21 Which of the following is **NOT** a complete sentence?

⬭ Sentence 4

⬭ Sentence 5

⬭ Sentence 6

⬭ Sentence 8

TEKS 3.22C

22 Which sentence does **NOT** belong in this report?

⬭ Sentence 5

⬭ Sentence 6

⬭ Sentence 7

⬭ Sentence 9

TEKS 3.17D

23 What is the **BEST** way to combine sentences 11 and 12?

⬭ In some schools, the boys sat on one side of the room and the girls sat on the other side.

⬭ In some schools, the boys and girls sat on the side.

⬭ In some schools the boys sat on one side of the room so the girls sat on the other side of the room.

⬭ The boys sat on one side of the room the girls sat on one side of the room.

TEKS 3.22A

GO ON

24 The meaning of sentence 13 can be improved by changing *they* to —

○ the teacher

○ that student

○ it

○ her

TEKS 3.17C

25 What is the **BEST** way to rewrite the ideas in sentence 15?

○ The other children sat quietly.

○ The other children were not reading or writing.

○ The other children sat quietly reading their books or writing their lessons.

○ The other children sat and read books.

TEKS 3.17C

26 What change, if any, should be made in sentence 16?

○ Change *me* to **I**

○ Change the period to a question mark

○ Change *would* to **wood**

○ Make no change

TEKS 3.23D

27 What change, if any, should be made in sentence 17?

○ Change *As to me* to **As for me**

○ Change *don't* to **do'nt**

○ Change *I'd* to **Id**

○ Make no change

TEKS 3.22A

28 What change, if any, should be made in sentence 18?

○ Change the question mark to a period

○ Delete the comma

○ Change *wed* to **we'd**

○ Make no change

TEKS 3.23C

STOP